THE COOL GUIDE TO EDINBURGH

THE COOL GUIDE TO EDINBURGH

Caroline Young

Photos by Martina Salvi

This edition published in 2013 by:

Thistle Publishing
36 Great Smith Street
London
SW1P 3BU

ISBN-13: 978-1-909869-17-2

CONTENTS

The National Monument on Calton Hill, lit up during Beltane

INTRODUCTION

Edinburgh is a city where dark and twisted history comes to life. It's rough, yet gentrified, friendly yet aloof, sophisticated and sexy, yet with a mysterious edge.

It's a small, intimate town that is easy to walk around and to get to know. It's a city where the locals can be incredibly friendly, but then tell their guests, as the old saying goes, 'you'll have had your tea.'

Edinburgh is a gothic wonderland of dark spires cutting through the often grey and foreboding sky. It's a city of dank closes, cobbled streets and sweeping vistas; a city that has inspired countless writers including the classic (Robert Burns, Sir Walter Scott, Robert Louis Stevenson) and the modern (Irvine Welsh, Kate Atkinson, David Nichols). But it also has a divide between the rich and poor. From the Georgian mansions and wealthy financiers to the areas of Leith, Niddry or Pilton, with their drug problems and

1

poverty that are a world away from the propriety of Morningside and the privileges of Edinburgh University students.

It's a city with a rich history, and with an old town built on many different layers, so you go up the Fleshmarket, down to the Cowgate and around the castle, which majestically holds court in the middle of the city. There are the crooked closes and alleyways of the Old Town to get lost in; cobbled terraces, the hidden vaults underneath the Bridges, steep streets and hills offering sweeping views over the city and to Fife.

Then there's the Georgian New Town, planned out in the 18th century to relieve the over-crowding of the Old Town. Princes Street Gardens was formed under the Castle after draining the surrounding loch, and many neo-classical buildings were built up as part of the Enlightenment, creating a city of learning, education and the arts. And how many cities boast a castle, a volcano and a beach?

Edinburgh also has an international flavour with its Polish convenience stores, Indian restaurants and a small Thai community, but is also distinctively Scottish, and that's not just the bagpipes and tartan down the Royal Mile.

But everybody has their own memories of the city carved into the cityscape. Childhood memories of chocolate ice-cream from DeLuca at the seaside turn into teenage nights wandering the Cowgate, ears pierced in Whip Lash Trash on Cockburn Street and buying vintage coats from Armstrongs. Then drinking in the pubs of Leith, and dancing to techno in the dark cavernous vaults under the bridges of the Old Town.

Edinburgh is Irn Bru mornings on Leith Walk with a Scottish breakfast. It's a sunny May Day stretched out on the grass in the Meadows with the rest of the city, catching this burst of sunshine that we almost forgot about as we survived another cold, foggy winter.

It's a city marked by the seasons. The smell of bonfire smoke and dampness in autumn, the city lit up with Christmas lights over the festive season, the glimmer of sunshine and hope in spring and then the stampede of festivals and events over summer.

It was local boys The Proclaimers who sang about the Sunshine on Leith. And when the sun reflects in the water of Leith, it prettifies what used to once be a seedy, dirty area. There are the old wrought iron lamps and cobbled streets of the Shore, with the quaint atmosphere of a sailors' port gone up market, but still with that rough underside.

Leith. Once the drinking den of sailors and prostitutes, and the setting for Irvine Welsh's Trainspotting, has been cleaned up in recent years. But its unofficial twinning with Rio de Janeiro seems perfectly fitting for its celebratory nature, a place where you can strike up a conversation with a stranger just by standing by the bar for a few minutes.

It mixes the old Leith and its dark underside, with new, upcoming, celebratory Leith. But don't worry, it's not completely cleaned up its act. Walking on Great Junction Street (or Great Junkie Street, as some people say) you can see a cast of many unusual characters as if they stepped out of an Irvine Welsh novel.

Edinburgh is a place that has inspired films and books and TV series. Alexander McCall Smith writes about the middle classes of the New Town, while Ian Rankin's Rebus explores the darker side. Then there's the Arthur's Seat of One Day and the cafes of the gothic Old Town where Harry Potter was penned.

In the New Town there are countless independent art galleries, and hidden bars along the twisted cobbled streets, including one of the finest cocktail places in the city. That's the thing about Edinburgh, there's a bar for everyone. Those in the know can tell you which ones open at 6am, for the posties who've just finished their rounds.

So if you are planning a trip to Edinburgh, here is the essential guide to getting the most out of the city and seeing the parts that you didn't know existed. Enjoy reading over a bottle of Crabbie's ginger beer and soak up the atmosphere of a hidden Edinburgh, while discovering the coolest places to go beyond the wine bars of George Street.

The view over Waverley to North Bridge

THE DETAILS

Arriving in Edinburgh

By train
The main arrival point in Edinburgh is Waverley Station, with entrances from the east of Princes Street and onto Market Street. Some trains also stop at Haymarket, a two-minute journey to Waverley, and more convenient for Edinburgh's West End.

By bus
Edinburgh's bus station is in the city centre, just off St Andrew Square, with an entrance next door to Harvey Nichols. City Link travels to cities and towns across Scotland, while First Bus goes to more local destinations.

By plane
Edinburgh Airport is about 9 miles from the city centre, and a taxi will cost roughly £20 into town.

The easiest and cheapest way to get to and from the city centre is by bus. The Airlink (X100 run by Lothian Buses) leaves from Waverley Bridge and directly outside Departures at the airport and takes about 30 minutes depending on the traffic. It costs £3.50 for a single journey and £6 for an open return.

Getting around

Lothian Buses is the main transport system across the city, with a good network and high frequency of buses, although they tend to stop about 11.30pm. You can pick up maps and timetables from their travel shop on the corner of Market Street and Waverley Bridge, on Hanover Street or by visiting their website www.lothianbuses.com. You can also download the app Bus Tracker for up-to-the minute times.

All trips cost £1.50 whatever the length, or you can get a Day Saver ticket for £3.50 for unlimited journeys.

Edinburgh is also a very convenient and pleasant city for walking around, and you can also bike across the city on a network of cycle paths. Check the Cycling section for more details.

A new tram system is in the process of being built, but with years of delays, disruption from the construction and escalating costs, it's a contentious subject among residents. But you will see the tramlines laid out along Princes Street and in the West End.

Emergency numbers

Dial 999 for the Police, Fire or Ambulance if it's an emergency. 101 is the number to dial for a non-emergency.

Lost property can be collected at Police Headquarters on Fettes Avenue, near Stockbridge.

Newspapers and magazines

Edinburgh's leading paper is The Scotsman, which also covers news across Scotland. The Evening News, which comes out at lunchtime everyday, deals with more parochial stories, perhaps also giving some insight into Edinburgh's low crime rate.

The List is a Scottish magazine with details of events and things to do across Scotland, aimed at a young, cool crowd. It's the publication to refer to if you particularly want to find out about club nights and gigs.

The Skinny is a free, Edinburgh-based arts magazine also with listings of what's on in Edinburgh, reviews and interviews.

Drinking times

Most bars are open until 12am or 1am, while clubs generally stay open until 3am. During the festival this can extend to 3am for pubs and 5am for clubs.

If you are not ready to go to bed just yet, there are several pubs that open early, from about 6am. These include the Penny Black, 17 West Register Street, and the Scotsman Lounge on Cockburn Street.

It's legal to drink in public spaces in Edinburgh, which means that you can bring drinks into parks in the city, provided you clear up after yourself.

Smoking

It's illegal to smoke in public places indoors in Scotland, but many bars and clubs have a dedicated outside smoking area, and you are also able to smoke at outdoor seating. People tend to gather round the entrances of pubs to smoke but be warned that you could get fined up to £50 for dropping cigarette butts on the ground.

A SOUNDTRACK TO THE CITY

Here are the top tunes for creating the perfect soundtrack to your visit to Edinburgh.

Iggy Pop - Lust for Life
Make like Renton and Spud, and imagine a chase by the cops across Princes Street and down Calton Road to the sound of Iggy Pop.

Stanley Odd – Join the Club
Stanley Odd do Scottish hip-hop with social realism. Join the Club takes you on a tour through the pubs and clubs of Edinburgh, some long gone, some still here.

CAROLINE YOUNG

The Proclaimers – Sunshine on Leith
Down at the Shore on a sunny day you can see the light twinkling off the water and re-imagine the romanticism of this part of the city as seen by Charlie and Craig Reid.

The Braveheart theme – James Horner
Why not conjure up the feel of Scottish nationalism while listening to the theme from Braveheart as you stand on the Castle esplanade, taking in the city.

King Creosote – Here on my Own
King Creosote is a singer and songwriter from Fife whose song Here on my own, was used in the film Hallam Foe.

Boards of Canada – 1969
A Scottish electronic group from Edinburgh, 1969 would be good to listen to while taking in the view from Calton Hill.

Underworld – Born Slippy
Another song from Trainspotting which defined the 1990s.

Leftfield – Shallow Grave
Used in the opening scenes of Shallow Grave, recreate the moment while listening as you walk through the Georgian streets of the New Town.

The Fall - Edinburgh Man
Taken from post punk group The Fall's 1991 album Shift-Work, Edinburgh Man is all about longing to be back in the city.

The Easy Club – Auld Toon Shuffle
"Edinburgh toon has a nice distinction…the Auld Town shuffle and the New Town stride", sung the Easy Club in 1984.

THE BIG ATTRACTIONS

Edinburgh Castle

Castlehill, 0131 225 9846, ec.enquiries@scotland.gsi.gov.uk

www.edinburghcastle.gov.uk

Adults £16, child £9.60, Concession £12.80

October to March 9.30am to 5pm, April to September 9.30am to 6pm

The mother of all attractions, Edinburgh Castle is Scotland's most visited tourist site, a fortress that dominates the skyline from its position high up on Castle Rock.

While it is run by Historic Scotland, the castle is also home to the British army and has been occupied as a site since 9th century BC, and a royal castle from the reign of King David I in the 12th century.

Every August the Military Tattoo takes place on the Esplanade, parading Scottish regiments and performers from around the world. And every day at 1pm, you'll hear a loud bang in the city centre. It's the One O Clock gun, fired since 1861 as a time signal for ships in the Firth of Forth.

Holyrood Palace

Canongate, 0131 556 5100

www.royalcollection.org.uk/visit/palaceofholyroodhouse

Jan to March 09.30am to 4.30pm, Apr to Oct 09.30am to 6pm, Nov to Dec 9.30am to 4.30pm

Check their website to find the days they are closed.

Adults £11, Concession £10, child £6.65, family ticket £29.25

The Queen's royal residence in Edinburgh, she visits during Holyrood Week from the end of June to beginning of July and holds her annual tea party in the grounds. The Palace dates back as an abbey built by David I in 1128, and was converted into a palace by James IV. Mary Queen of Scots came to live in the palace in 1562 and Bonnie Prince Charlie seized control in 1745, becoming the symbolic home of the Stuart line. Explore the ornate rooms of this palace, which was a particular favourite home for Queen Victoria.

The Scottish Parliament
Horse Wynd, 0131 348 5000
www.scottish.parliament.uk
Monday, Friday and Saturday 10am to 5pm, Tuesday to Thursday 10am to 6pm, Sunday Closed
Tours of the building are free, but the building is closed on Sundays and tours are only available on Tuesday, Wednesdays and Thursdays when parliament is in recess. Visit the website to book in advance.

One of Scotland's more modern controversies, the Scottish Parliament was finely completed in 2004, three years late and about £400 million over budget, and with great criticism of the location, the appointment of a non-Scottish architect and the design of the building itself.

The idea for a new Scottish Parliament came about after devolution in 1997. Scottish Members of Parliament argue decisions of the country in the debating chamber, there are committee rooms and it also houses office and administrative staff.

As for the building, some love it, some hate it, but you can see the influence of the Catalan architect Enric Miralles who sadly died before completion. The modernist, abstract design does have a resemblance to buildings in Barcelona, but its aim, with its iconography, is to link with the Scottish landscape and culture. Some of the features include cube-like windows inspired by Henry Raeburn's painting, The Skating Minister, leaf-shaped roof lights, timber trigger panels on the outside, and Scottish quotations inscribed on the Canongate wall.

It has won numerous awards, including the 2005 Stirling Prize, which is the UK's most prestigious award for architecture. See what you think of it yourself by taking one of the free tours.

Arthur's Seat

Holyrood Park Education Centre

1 Queen's Drive, 0131 652 8150, hs.rangers@scotland.gsi.gov.uk

www.historic-scotland.gov.uk

Arthur's Seat is a dormant volcano right in the middle of the city, which many people say resembles a sleeping lion. It was described by Robert Louis Stevenson as "a hill for magnitude, a mountain in virtue of its bold design."

There are several ways to climb to the top, either the route along the ridge, known as Salisbury Crag, or a brisk walk up the grassy verge, but you get sweeping views right across the city and over the Firth of Forth. There are also lots of paths to explore in and around the park. Historic Scotland's ranger service who look after Holyrood Park often provide guided tours on the geological history and early settlements. Call into the Holyrood Park Education Centre to find out more.

See the Outdoors section for more information on Holyrood Park.

Edinburgh Zoo

134 Corstorphine Road, 0131 334 9171, info@rzss.org.uk

Adults £16, child £11.50, Concession £13.50

Apr to Sep 9am to 6pm, Oct and Mar 9am to 5pm, Nov to Feb 9am to 4.30pm

Everybody loves pandas and Edinburgh zoo is home to the UK's only giant pandas, a gift from China with hopes of breeding. They've really been celebrated in the city, with some banners up in nearby Corstorphine, and a Panda Cam to watch them live. The penguins are also famous for their parade around the zoo, first introduced in 1914, and you can get close to the chimps at the Budongo trail. The Zoo celebrated 100 years in 2013, and has been praised by Sir David Attenborough as the model zoo. They have lots of great events for kids and hold adults only zoo nights with silent disco, champagne and performers. It's worth looking at their website to see what events they have coming up.

The Forth Rail Bridge

The rust red cantilever railway bridge, spanning the Firth of Forth, was built in 1890 and is considered one of the world's greatest feats of engineering.

It's 2,465 metres long, 150m high and uses 10 times as much steel as the Eiffel Tower. Before the bridge was built, people would have to get a ferry over to Fife to link up with the rest of Scotland or go the long way round via Stirling. Construction began in 1883 and cost the lives of 63 men, although countless more were seriously injured. It's also said that the painting of the bridge is a never ending job – by the time it's completed, painting will have to start again.

You can cross over it by jumping on one of the many trains going to Fife, such as on the Dunfermline route, and the best point for viewing it is by the waterfront at South Queensferry.

There are opportunities to abseil 165 feet down the structure, usually through an event organized by a charity like Chest, Heart and Stroke Scotland and Deaf Blind Scotland.

The Royal Botanic Garden Edinburgh
Inverleith Place Lane, 0131 552 7171
www.rbge.org.uk
Mar to Sept 10am to 6pm, Nov to Jan 10am to 4pm, Feb and Oct 10am to 5pm
Free entry
The Botanics is one of the most relaxing places in the city to go for a wander, to enjoy the tropical hothouse, and to get great views over to the Castle. The recently built welcome centre, The John Hope Gateway, is an interesting sustainable structure with shop, exhibitions, and labs carrying out botany and scientific research. The Botanics was originally established in 1670 near Holyrood Palace, and moved to Inverleith in 1820. The Palm House, built in 1858, is the tallest in the UK. There's a rock garden to jump over, a heath garden, redwoods, a Chinese hillside, footpaths to explore 13,300 different species of plant, many of which were collected from exotic empire outposts, and a lot of squirrels.

The National Museum of Scotland

The National Museum of Scotland
Chambers Street, 0300 123 6789
www.nms.ac.uk
Everyday 10am to 5pm, free entry
The National Museum of Scotland is a treasure-trove of art and national history. Some of the Scottish treasures include 11 of the Lewis Chessman, flags from the Battle of Culedon, sculptures by Sir Eduardo Paolazzo, Pictish stones and Celtic decorative art. The giant whale-skeleton suspended from the ceiling is also a favourite.

The original museum was opened in 1888 and designed by the man behind the Royal Albert Hall in London, Captain Francis Fowke. The huge Victorian entrance hall with its cast ironwork and cupola was recently refurbished, and the modern sandstone extension, opened in 1998, has exhibitions that chart Scotland's history.

The Museum of Childhood
42 High Street, 0131 529 5152
www.edinburghmuseums.org.uk
Monday to Saturday 1am to 5pm, Sunday 12pm to 5pm, Entrance is free
The Museum of Childhood can be quite a nostalgia trip, depending on how old you are! They have all sorts of toys from the past on display – Barbie dolls, teddy bears, action figures, board games, books and comics. There's an interactive 1930s schoolroom, a replica Victorian Street and a chance for kids to dress up in old clothing.

Surgeons' Hall Museums
Nicolson Street, 0131 527 1711, museum@rcsed.ac.uk
www.museum.rcsed.ac.uk
Everyday 10am to 5pm
Surgeons' Hall, one of the largest collections of surgical pathology in the world, has some weird and wonderful artefacts and specimens and displays from centuries of pathology, dentistry and surgery, from The Royal College of Surgeons, established in 1505. 19th century plaster casts of facial tumours, a collection of skeletons suffering genetic abnormalities, some scary looking dentistry equipment and William Burke's death mask are some of the items on display. In the garden of the museum is a menacing statue of a hand brandishing a saw.

Our Dynamic Earth
112-116 Holyrood Road, 0131 550 7800
Adult £11.50, concession £9.75, children £7.50
Everyday 10am to 5.30pm (November to February closed Mondays and Tuesdays) July and August open until 6pm
Next door to the Scottish Parliament, Our Dynamic Earth was specially built in 1999 as a science centre in a tent-like structure. It explores the evolution of the planet, from dinosaurs to rainforest, to the depth of ocean and into space, through interactive exhibits and 3D and 4D shows. They do special talks and exhibitions and host events during the annual Edinburgh International Science Festival in spring.

Museum of Edinburgh

142 – 146 Canongate, 0131 529 4143

www.edinburghmuseums.org.uk

Monday to Saturday 10am to 5pm, Sunday 12pm to 5pm (August only) Free entry

If you want to find out the history of Edinburgh, then Museum of Edinburgh, in a late 16th century house on the Royal Mile, explores the origins and stories behind the city. Their collection included an original copy of the National Covenant, James Craig's plans for the New Town, and Greyfriars Bobby's collar and bowl. Huntley House is an interesting building in itself, with creaking floorboards, tight staircases, a maze of rooms and a nice courtyard. Their newest attraction, Foundation Edinburgh, is a light display that takes you on a journey through Edinburgh's history.

Camera Obscura and World of Illusions

Castlehill, 0131 226 3709, info@camera-obscura.co.uk

www.camera-obscura.co.uk

July and August 9.30am to 9pm everyday, November to March 10am to 6pm everyday, April to June, September, October 9.30am to 7pm everyday

Adult £11.95, concession £9.95, children £8.75

One of Edinburgh's oldest attractions, Camera Obscura has been going for 150 years, and is basically the original Victorian version of Google maps - capturing live images of Edinburgh through mirrors, lenses and light. It's in the original 'Outlook' tower, bought by townplanner Patrick Geddes, who took people up the tower and showed them the Camera Obscura, to give them a different outlook in life. You can get a great rooftop view from the tower over the Old Town, and there is also The World of Illusions, which has interactive exhibits and illusions.

The Real Mary King's Close

2 Warriston's Close, High Street, 0845 070 6244

www.realmarykingsclose.com

November to March, Sunday to Thursday 10am to 5pm, Friday and Saturday 10am to 9pm

March to October, everyday 10am to 9pm

Adults £12.95, Concession £11.45, Child £7.45. (Not suitable for children under 5)

A real, spooky Edinburgh experience for exploring a hidden under-ground street dating back to the middle ages, covered up for centuries after an outbreak of the plague. Edinburgh's Old Town was built up on many different layers, and Mary King's Close was once a bustling street out in the open. It was buried under the City Chambers and only opened to the public a decade ago. Actors dressed up in 17th century costume will take you through some scenarios to bring the story to light as you travel through subterranean chambers that could well be haunted with the ghosts of trapped souls.

Gilmerton Cove

16 Drum Street, bookings@gilmertoncove.org.uk, 0845 894 5295

www.gilmertoncove.org.uk

It's only available by appointment, but you can arrange a time between 10am and 4pm, for an hour-long tour.

Adult £7.50, child 5-16 £4, Concession £6.50, family ticket £20

Gilmerton Cove is a mysterious series of hand-carved tunnels and chambers beneath the former coal-mining village of Gilmerton, in South Edinburgh, which opened as a tourist attraction in 2003. You can access it through the visitor centre in an old mining cottage. No one is quite sure what the passageways were built for, but some of the theories are that it was a secret gentlemen's drinking den, a smuggler's lair or a haven for persecuted Covenanters. There's also a possible link with the Knights Templar.

Not suitable for under 5 years old or wheelchair users because of the uneven ground.

Royal Yacht Britannia

Access inside the shopping centre Ocean Terminal, Ocean Drive, 0131 555 5566, enquiries@tryb.co.uk

www.royalyachtbritannia.co.uk

Adult £12, children £7.50, concession £10.50, Family ticket £35

Jan, Feb, Mar, Nov, Dec 10am to 3.30pm, Apr, May, Jun, Oct 9.30am to 4pm, Jul, Augu, Sept, 9.30am to 4.30pm

Find out what life was like for the Windsor's when they took to the high seas, by visiting The Royal Yacht Britannia, at its berth in Leith. The ship was home on the Ocean for the Royal Family for 44 years, after being launched by the Queen in 1953. Her father King George VI died 2 days after commissioning the yacht in 1952, so the Queen had the final say in the design, still preserved. Charles and Diana and Prince Andrew and Fergie spent their Honeymoons on board and the Queen and Prince Philip travelled to exotic, far-flung places on state visits. You get a glimpse of 1950s Royal style with the original art and décor, or have tea, scones or champagne on the deck, where the Royals would've held drinks receptions for such guests as Winston Churchill, Nelson Mandela and Ronald Reagan.

Easter Road Stadium and Tynecastle Stadium
Tynecastle Stadium, McLeod Street, 0871 663 1874
Easter Road Stadium, 12 Albion Place, 0131 661 2159
Hearts and Hibs are Edinburgh's two football teams, and you can pick your allegiance by visiting either of their stadiums. There's a somewhat healthy rivalry between the two teams, less than the ferocity between the fans of Glasgow's Celtic and Rangers teams. The Edinburgh darby between the two teams is said to be one of the oldest football rivalries in the world.

Hibernian football club, founded in 1875, is traditionally North Edinburgh and Catholic, and the stadium is just off Easter Road, which runs parallel to Leith Walk. Fans get called Hibees, and the strip is green and white, reflecting the Irish heritage.

Heart of Midlothian, dating back to 1873, is based at Tynecastle Stadium in Gorgie, in the South West of the city. Hearts supporters are nicknamed Jambos (rhyming jam tarts for hearts) and the strip is maroon and white. The name comes from the Heart of Midlothian on the Royal Mile.

The Scott Monument
East Princes Street Gardens, 0131 529 4068, museumcollections@edinburgh.gov.uk
www.edinburghmueums.org.uk
April to September, Monday to Saturday 10am to 7pm, Sunday 10am to 6pm
October to March Monday to Saturday 9am to 4pm, Sunday 10am to 6pm
Admission£4

The Scott Monument

The world's largest monument to a writer, Sir Walter Scott, The Scott Monument juts out from Princes Street Gardens, with the resemblance of a small Eiffel Tower or a gothic, multi-tiered wedding cake. There are 287 steps to the top, it's 61 metres high, and the design features 64 statues from the works of Scott. Architect George Meike Kemp based his gothic design on Melrose Abbey and Rosslyn Chapel, and it was completed in 1846.

Princes Street Gardens
November to February 7am to 5pm, March, April, September and October 7am to 7pm, May and June 7am to 8pm, July and August 7am to 10pm

One of the most beautiful places to visit in Edinburgh, Princes Street Gardens lies in the shadow of the Castle and Edinburgh Rock. It features the Scott Monument and the Grecian-style National Galleries of Scotland, grassy slopes, shady spots beneath the trees, flower beds, lots of squirrels and a little network of paths that go across the gardens and over the railway line that cuts through.

It's divided into the east and west gardens, and during December and the beginning of January the east gardens are converted into the Winter Wonderland, with ice-rink, funfair and German market.

The west gardens have little shelters along the footpath, the Ross Bandstand where big-name acts perform on Hogmanay, a cute gardener's cottage, and a carrousel and Ross fountain at the far side.

Also in West Princes Street Gardens, just by the entrance on the Mound, is the Floral Clock with a very charming Cuckoo Clock, which pops out on the hour. The clock has been going since 1903 and the pattern of the floral clock is based around a different theme each year, celebrating everything from the centenary of The Girl Guides to the Territorial Army.

Calton Hill
Calton Hill can be accessed by walking up Waterloo Place, via Royal Terrace or up Regent's Road.

Calton Hill, a volcanic rock with excellent views across the city, used to have a reputation as a gay pick-up spot, and for being a little dangerous at nighttime. More recently the pagan Beltane Festival takes place at the end

THE COOL GUIDE TO EDINBURGH

of April every year, and it's also a popular spot for watching the fireworks on Hogmanay and at the end of the festival.

There are lots of monuments to explore up on Calton Hill, many in the Greek Revivalist style as part of a 19th century plan to fulfil Edinburgh's Athens of the North status with its own Acropolis. It was to be a symbol of the Enlightment movement, a wave of Scottish intellectualism during that period.

The Old City Observatory, designed by William Playfair in 1818, was inspired by a Greek temple of the Four Winds, and offers a history of 19th century astronomy with original telescopes on display.

The Dugald Stewart Monument, built in tribute to Scottish philosopher Dugald Stewart, was built in 1831 and its design by William Playfair was based on the Choragic Monument of Lysicrates in Athens. This also inspired the Robert Burns monument, built at the same time.

The Old Royal High School was modelled on the Hephaisteion in Athens, and was used as a school building from 1826 to 1968, before the school moved to Barnton in west Edinburgh.

The never-completed National Monument was once described as 'Edinburgh's disgrace' after a lack of funds meant it could never be completed, and work was stopped in 1829. It was based on the Parthenon in Athens, and built as a tribute to fallen soldiers during the Napoleonic Wars.

Nelson Monument was completed in 1815, designed in tribute to Lord Nelson, who died at the Battle of Trafalgar. It features a timeball, which was dropped at 1 o'clock so that sailors could work out the exact time. The ritual is still a daily occurrence, except for Sundays.

The Political Martyrs' Monument is a sandstone obelisk constructed in 1844, and in tribute to five political figures – Thomas Muir, Thomas Fyshe Palmer, William Skirving, Maurice Margarot and Joseph Gerrald.

You can also rent a room in the Old Observatory House – one of the more unique places to stay in the city. (see Places to Sleep).

Jenners
48 Princes Street, 0844 800 3725
Monday to Saturday 10am to 7pm (Thursday open until 8pm), Sunday 11am to 6.30pm

London may have Harrods and Selfridges, but Edinburgh has Jenners. Founded in 1838, and given the Royal seal of approval, Jenners was Scotland's oldest independent store until it was bought over by House of Frasers. The original building was destroyed by fire, but the ornate building that stands there now was opened in 1895 and is a category A listed building, with the columns of sculpted female figures around the outside supposedly representing women's support of the household.

The Scotsman Steps

Ground entrance on Market Street

These enclosed steps by the Scotsman Hotel link the Old and New Towns, and act as a shortcut from North Bridge down to the entrance of Waverley Station. It was an access point for The Scotsman newspaper when it occupied the building that is now the hotel, but the steps fell into disrepair, being used as an unofficial toilet stop for drunk people falling out of nearby nightclubs.

The steps have now become an artwork by Scottish artist Martin Creed, Work No 1059, as commissioned by the neighbouring the Fruitmarket Gallery. He encased each step in different coloured marble from around the globe, which Creed has said represents a microcosm of the world.

Lauriston Castle

2 Cramond Road South, 0131 336 2060

http://www.edinburghmuseums.org.uk/Venues/Lauriston-Castle.aspx

One hour tours: April to October, Monday to Thursday, Saturday and Sunday 2pm;November to March, Saturday and Sunday 2pm

No need to book

Adult £5, Children £3, Concessions £3

For fans of Downton Abbey, Lauriston Castle gives you a real insight into the upstairs and downstairs of a wealthy Edwardian home. The house dates back to the 16th century, with an 18th century extension, but was bought by the Reid family in 1903. They completely redecorated the interior with antiques, framed tapestry and Edwardian pieces, such as ultra-fashionable tropical motifs. There are doors hidden within bookcases and a secret passage into a turret that was used for listening into conversations in the study. The Reid's also had all the mod-cons of the day, including electricity, central heating, a seated flush toilet and a shower. The house sits in large grounds, and there is a Japanese garden gifted by Kyoto, one of the cities twinned with Edinburgh. The website has all the details of events they organise including a Murder Mystery evening.

Calton Hill at dusk

The Meadows

THE GREAT OUTDOORS

Edinburgh is packed with places to get some fresh air, from large parks to wilderness areas in the city, ideal for taking a break from the traffic and the concrete.

Edinburgh is said to be built on seven hills, and each one is a little sanctuary of escapism. Every June the Seven Hills Race challenges people to run up each of the hills – Arthur's Seat, Castle Rock, Calton Hill, Corstorphine Hill, Braid Hills and Corstorphine Hill - choosing your own route. But if that sounds a bit too much, here are some picks for the best places to get out in the fresh air for activities, walking or just relaxing.

Holyrood Park
It's incredible to have this huge royal park with a volcano (Arthur's Seat), three lochs (St Margaret's Loch, Dunsapie Loch, and Duddingston Loch), glens and a ruined abbey, only a blink from the Scottish Parliament and the Royal Mile.

It was originally a 12th century hunting grounds, before James V enclosed the area with a stone wall to set aside as royal estate. Arthur's Seat is the highest point in Edinburgh at 823 feet. It's an easy climb up by various different routes, but one of the most popular s is via Salisbury Crags, that runs aside high cliffs. 15th century St Anthony's Chapel is the picturesque ruin overlooking St Margaret's Loch, a former marsh converted into a loch by Prince Albert in 1856, with geese, swans and ducks. There are also remains of prehistoric cultivation terraces on the east side of Arthur's Seat.

To find out about all the walks you should do, and details of archaeology check out www.historic-scotland.gov.uk.

The Meadows
Everybody and their dog comes to the Meadows over the summer. It's a huge park in the southside, very near Edinburgh University, where people cycle and jog along tree-lined Middle Meadow walk, have barbeques, drink some beers, kick a ball about or practice slack-lining. There's a playground, croquet club, tennis courts and cricket facilities, the Pavilion Café for grabbing a coffee, and on a weekend in June it's taken over by the Meadows Festival. Look out for the archway made from a whale's jawbones, which had been displayed during an 1886 science festival.

The Hermitage of Braid and Blackford Hill Local Nature Reserve
In the south of the city, the top of Blackford Hill has some good views over Edinburgh and to the Pentland Hills. There's good wildlife spotting at the pond, and the Royal Observatory, near the summit, has talks on Monday evenings and holds astronomy events during winter. Interesting fact - the Royal Observatory and its big copper domes were bombed by the Suffragette movement in May 1913.

The city's park rangers are based at the old 18th century Hermitage House in The Hermitage of Braid, a woodland wildlife reserve. At their visitor centre you can find out about the activities and events that they regularly hold. Within the Braid there's a wildflower meadow near the Braid Road entrance and a walled garden near the doocot, which is an old pigeon house. There are also plenty of relaxing walks within the reserve.

Inverleith Park
This huge park in North Edinburgh has sweeping views over the New Town and up to the Castle and Arthur's Seat. There's also a running trail around the perimeter with exercise pit-stops for doing push-ups, pull-ups and other old-school exercises on wooden frames. There's a sundial garden, a duck pond and rows of allotments.

Burdiehouse Burn Valley Park
This little known reserve in south Edinburgh, which follows the burn as it snakes through several housing estates, has woodland walks, a wildflower meadow, a small skatepark, cycletracks and makes a peaceful escape from the

city. There are several entrances – accessible by Gilmerton Road or Ellen's Glen Road.

The Union Canal

The Union Canal goes 35 miles from Fountainbridge in Edinburgh out to Falkirk, and you can follow the footpath alongside it, or hire a canoe for some of the way. The canal was built to transport coal into the city and there are several amazing aqueducts along the way – the Almond Aqueduct near Ratho, and the Avon Aqueduct near Linlithgow, which at 810 feet is the second longest in the UK.

If you are with a large group, you could explore the Union Canal on a barge hired from Re-Union Canal Boats in Fountainbridge.

www.re-union.org.uk, 1 Union Path, 0131 261 8529, info@re-union.org.uk

On Sundays you can hire a boat from Edinburgh Canal Society's boathouse on Ashley Terrace, near Harrison Park.

Corstorphine Hill

Corstorphine Hill, near Edinburgh Zoo, is a woodland area with lots of different paths to explore. Corstorphine Hill tower was built as a memorial to Sir Walter Scott and there's a community walled garden, with a claim to fame of having featured on the TV programme The Beechgrove Garden. Barnton Quarry (now undergoing a restoration project - www.barntonquarry. org.uk) was a Second World War radar centre and then a cold war nuclear bunker. There are several entrances to this park, from Clermiston Road and Queensferry Road.

www.corstorphinehill.org.uk

The Water of Leith

One of the most romantic walks in Edinburgh is along the Water of Leith, the main river that runs through Edinburgh. You can follow the 35km journey from the Pentland Hills and down to Leith, or dip in and out of the route. The walk takes you past old mills, under bridges, through tunnels and past historical monuments. You can also spot herons, swans and kingfisher, while brown trout and eels live in the water.

www.waterofleith.org.uk

Cramond Island

Cramond

Cramond is a little village down on the Firth of Forth, with a rocky beach and promenade to explore the shoreline. You can walk out to Cramond Island via the causeway, but be warned – check the tide times as the causeway is submerged by water when the tide is high. There have been groups of people who have been stranded on the island after miscalculating. 15th Century Cramond kirk and a stone sculpture of a fish by Ronald Rae are also worth a look.

The Pentland Hills
The Pentland Hills, straddled between Edinburgh and West Lothian, is easy to get to by bus (Lothian buses 10 and 16 go there) and with 100km of walking trails, hills dotted with sheep farms, gorges and woodland, there are opportunities for fishing, camping, walking and cycling. Because of the altitude it gets very snowy during winter, and Midlothian Snowsports Centre is a dry ski slope for all year round skiing. (www.midlothian.gov.uk/info/200131/snowsports_centre/)

The Flotterstone Information Centre, near the Flotterstone Inn, or the Harlaw House Visitor Centre near Currie are good places to get started as they have maps and guided trails. MacEwen's buses has a service that goes from Edinburgh bus station to Flotterstone Inn, while Lothian Bus 44 goes to Currie, where you can then walk to Harlaw visitor centre.
www.pentlandhills.org

Saughton Park
Saughton Park has Edinburgh's only skatepark, with 2,100 square metres of concrete bowls, designed in conjunction with a group of Edinburgh skaters and riders. Local graffiti artists were also involved in creating art and logos. The park also has running tracks, football pitches and a winter garden to explore.
www.edinburghskatepark.org.uk

CYCLING IN EDINBURGH

The old railway lines in Edinburgh have long been out of use, but after being paved over, they have become popular cycle routes throughout Edinburgh, creating 75km of paths across the city.

You can pretty much get anywhere in the city using these paths. The inner tube map, designed to look like the London underground, details these paths and how to get to one side of the city to the other while avoiding traffic. www.innertubemap.com

One of the highlights is the Innocent Railway tunnel, a 517-metre long tunnel under Holyrood Park which connects south and east Edinburgh. The line was called 'Innocent' because of its record of having no accidents, but the tunnel is damp, dark and can be quite spooky.

The promenade is also a good cycle route, stretching 17km from Cramond to Joppa along the Firth of Forth and passing through Granton, Newhaven and Leith.

You could continue on along the Lothian coastline, passing through the seaside towns of Musselburgh and North Berwick. You could stop at the beach at Luffness, explore the rocky coastline by Gullane, and enjoy some cake at Falko Konditorei at 1 Stanley Road in Gullane. Continue on to North Berwick and you could go back to Edinburgh via the historic town, Haddington.

The Vat Run in South Queensferry is a mountainbike trail and pump track that has been built by a team of volunteers. Their work is still ongoing to create a series of trails for biking. Visit thevatrun.co.uk to find out their progress.

Glentress Forest, 30 miles south of Edinburgh, is a mecca of mountainbiking trails through beautiful woodland and hillside. There is a mix of trails for different abilities, and a free ride park for practicing jumps, but a 30km black grade trail has been voted one of the best in Britain. www.glentressforest.com

For more detailed routes and maps around Edinburgh, try cycle charities Spokes and Sustrans. www.spokes.org.uk and www.sustrans.org.uk

Here are some suggestions for where to hire a bike – each place also provides helmet, bike lock and cycle kit.

Grease Monkey Cycles
0845 180 1251
www.greasemonkeycycles.com
They offer half-day hire for £19 and full day hire for £26, with free delivery in Edinburgh.

Leith Cycle Co
276 Leith Walk, 0131 467 7775, leith@leithcycleco.com
Half day bike hire for £12 and a full day for £17.

Bike Trax
11 – 13 Lochrin Place, 0131 228 6633, info@biketrax.co.uk
www.biketrax.co.uk
They hire city and road bikes for £17 a day.

Tara Nowy. Photo by Elliott Mackie

TARA NOWY, MODEL AND DAUGHTER OF MARILLION FRONT-MAN FISH.

What's your fondest childhood memory of Edinburgh?

It would definitely be a day trip I had with my granddad when I was around 9 years old. I had never properly seen Edinburgh before but I just remember roaming the cobbled streets and being told stories such as that of Greyfriars Bobby, visiting the museum and having a tea and scone in the cafe. It's probably when I realised how magical Edinburgh is.

If you had 24 hours in the city what would you do?

It's dependant on the time of year, because in August I would just be trawling the different shows! But any other time I would definitely advise just having a wander and take in the beautiful city. There are so many gorgeous shops and little cafes and often art exhibitions.

The Brass Monkey is always great for a sneaky pint, it really has that old man pub vibe which I love. It's quite close to the museum which is free and also near the Elephant House, the birthplace of Harry Potter. If you prefer a great coffee and some of the most amazing bread and German cakes including Baum Kuchen then head to Falko on Bruntsfield Place.

At night there are often live gigs on. A favourite place for me to go to is Whistle Binkies. I have seen some great talent there like the Victorian Trout Conspiracy, or The Jazz Bar for a more chilled out night.

Where's your favourite place to buy clothes?

It would probably have to be Armstrongs. It's a complete and utter treasure trove! I can spend hours sifting through the rails. For hats it would definitely be Joyce Paton's Boutique. Her designs are absolutely stunning and can also be found in Jane Davidson on Thistle Street, another go to store for a carefully selected collection of pieces from designers such as Missoni, Dries van Noten and Diane von Furstenberg.

What would be your perfect Friday night?

Catching up with friends in somewhere like Joseph Pearce on Elm Row. It's great for 'sun-downers', then maybe a meal in a Japanese restaurant. I would follow that with a live gig or a boogie in Cabaret Voltaire, which is probably my favourite club in Edinburgh. But if I fancy something a little more grimey, Sneaky Pete's is my go to club.

Favourite place for food?

Sushi is my absolute favourite, hands down. I could eat it every day for the rest of my life and never get sick. Sushiya by Haymarket is literally a cupboard but does a fantastic tataki. Yes Sushi on Hannover Street is excellent and good value, while Kampai is a bit more expensive but a lovely place to take a date.

If I am having a day where all I want is meat and carbs then I go to Oink on Victoria Street for a big juicy pork-packed roll topped with apple sauce. You can't miss it as they have a whole roast pig in the window!

To get some fresh air, where would you go?

I used to live on Montrose Terrace which is right by Calton Hill, and loved going for walks around there. It's a fabulous area with Arthur's Seat nearby and a short walk from the city centre. My favourite view of Edinburgh is on Regent Road, standing by the Burns Monument, it just seems that little but more magical.

The Witchery. Photo courtesy of The Witchery

Hotel Missoni. Photo courtesy of Missoni

Dakota Edinburgh, courtesy of Dakota Hotels

Old Observatory House Hotel, photo courtesy of Vivat Trust

PLACES TO SLEEP

Iconic

The Balmoral Hotel
1 Princes Street, 0131 556 2414, reservations.balmoral@roccofortehotels.com
www.thebalmoralhotel.com
A baroque icon at the end of Princes Street and North Bridge, the Balmoral Hotel was once known as the Great British Hotel until the 1980s, built as the hotel for Waverley Station, and the original features are preserved and enhanced, for stately, turn of the century style. There's a popular afternoon tea held in Colonial-styled Palm Court, with a harpist playing on the balcony as champagne, sandwiches and cakes are served. The restaurant, Number One, is one of the five Michelin starred restaurants in city.

The Scotsman Hotel
20 North Bridge, 0131 556 5565
www.thescotsmanhotel.co.uk
This five star hotel is in the former offices of the Scotsman newspapers, an ornate 1905 building on North Bridge, its location chosen for ease of getting the papers into Waverley Station for delivery. The Scotsman Hotel has kept and enhanced many of the Baroque features, including the marble staircase, marble pillars, and oak panelling of the reception area, which is now the bar and restaurant, and with the curved windows of the turrets in some of the bedrooms. The printing press on the lower ground floor has been converted into the health club and spa.

The Witchery by the Castle
Castlehill, 0131 225 5613, reservations@thewitchery.com
www.thewitchery.com
The Witchery, with its name inspired by the witches who were burnt at the stake at Castlehill, is a magical place that has attracted celebrities like Kate Moss. It's in the traditional sense of an inn, a restaurant with rooms attached, and located in a 16th century merchant's house in prime position next to the Castle. It's dark, gothic, opulent, with tapestries and gargoyles, and you almost expect designer cobwebs to be hanging off the chandelier. Rooms are decked out like a Tudor palace with four-poster beds, sweeping red velvet curtains, piles of cushions, brocade and antique furniture. The gothic windows of the neighbouring 19th century church that overlooks the courtyard adds to the atmosphere of devilish indulgence.

The Caledonian
Princes Street, 0131 222 8888, guest_caledonian@waldorfastoria.com
www.thecaledonianedinburgh.com
The Caley, in its grand red sandstone building at the top of Lothian Road, was built in 1903 as part of the Princes Street railway station, and was considerd the height of luxury when it opened. The station was closed in 1965 as Waverley Station was made the primary route, and the hotel was then extended, with the railway station concourse turned into a bar area. The Caley was bought over by Waldorf Astoria in 2012, but they have kept all the old features but have renamed the bar and café area Peacock Alley, in honour of the New York hotel.

Splurge

Prestonfield House
Priestfield Road, 0131 225 7800, reservations@prestonfield.com
www.prestonfield.com
Prestonfield is a luxury 5 star boutique in a 17th century house, decorated in a gothic, brocade, style with uniquely decorated rooms featuring huge antique beds, tapestries, gilded mirrors and plasma screens hidden away to keep a traditional feel. It's been a hotel for 50 years, but prior to that was a mansion

and estate with connections to royalty, particularly the Stuart line and Mary Queen of Scots. A previous owner in the 18ᵗʰ century was inspired by visits to Italy to paint neo-classical motifs onto panelling. Past guests have included Oliver Reed, Winston Churchill and Catherine Zeta Jones.

Hotel Du Vin
11 Bristo Place, 084473 642 55
www.hotelduvin.com
Intriguingly set in a converted lunatic asylum, Hotel Du Vin is a unique city centre hotel in a rambling old building. You enter through a stone tunnel, which opens up into a courtyard with tables lit with lanterns in the evenings. The décor in each room is traditional luxury with a rich colour scheme, clawfoot bathtubs and monsoon showers, tweed cushions, and a bar area with leather seats, lots of tartan and mahogany. They pay particular focus their selection of fine wines, with a brimming cellar and expert sommeliers to recommend something for each event in your stay.

Malmaison, the Shore
1 Tower Place, the Shore
www.malmaison.com
Malmaison occupies a building that was originally a sailor's home for recovery, first opened in 1885 and with a reputation for debauchery. It's in a prime position on The Shore and their rooms are decorated with a Scottish slant, some with four-poster beds and all the features you would expect. Madonna stayed here when the MTV video music awards took place in Edinburgh in 2003. The Brasserie has a relaxed, loungy feel with leather, wood and brick, and a menu of Scottish and Brit classics.

The Sheraton Grand Hotel and Spa
1 Festival Square, 0131 229 9131
www.sheratonedinburgh.co.uk
After being given a re-design last year, the Sheraton, in its slightly tatty concrete building on Festival Square, has a new contemporary Scottish design for its 269 comfy bedrooms, and you can do a £30 upgrade for a view of the

Castle. They've also introduced One Square as a more informal space, with a Jetsons styled bar that specialises in gin, and a claim to be the only hotel in Edinburgh to have a special club lounge. One Spa is the highlight of this complex.

Old Observatory House Hotel, Calton Hill
0845 090 0194, enquiries@vivat-trust.org
www.vivat-trust.org
Run by conservation charity Vivat Trust, the Old Observatory House Hotel is one of the most unique places to stay in Edinburgh. It can sleep eight people in four bedrooms over its three floors, and also has a sitting room, kitchen and a circular drawing room within the domed observatory. Every room has sweeping views across Edinburgh and over to Fife.

The Howard
34 Great King Street, 0131 557 3500, reserve@thehoward.com
www.theedinburghcollection.com
The 5 Star Howard has 18 rooms in three Georgian townhouses, close to Stockbridge and only ten minutes walk into town. It's a splendorous place, decorated in opulent New Town style with old-fashioned bathtubs, regal stripes, and opulent dining room with huge dining table.

The Glasshouse
2 Greenside Place, 0131 525 8200 resglasshouse@theetoncollection.co.uk
Directly behind Calton Hill, and in a converted church still with the stone façade, but with a glass extension behind it, the Glasshouse is a stylish boutique hotel, with eclectic décor and light filtering through the huge windows. One of their highlights is a roof terrace with amazing views across the city.

Missoni Hotel
George IV Bridge, 0131 220 6666, Edinburgh@hotelmissoni.com
www.hotelmissoni.com
Missoni striped fabrics may not be to everyone's taste, but this style hotel owned by the family Missoni keeps the branding of the design to every detail,

with the strapping guards at the door dressed in Missoni patterned kilts and the giant mosaic vases and thread spool in the lobby. The theme of the hotel incorporates Missoni monochrome with splashes of colour, Scottish touches such as the Charles Rennie Mackintosh chairs in reception, and bedrooms with Missoni bedspreads and cushions, Missoni homeware in the bar and restaurant, and framed original costume sketches by Missoni for a Scottish set opera in the 1980s. It's a fascinating place, just to take in the exact attention to even the tiniest details in keeping with the Italian brand.

Le Monde
16 George Street, 0131 270 3900, contact@lemondehotel.co.uk
www.lemondehotel.co.uk
Unashamedly snobby, Le Monde is for the ladies who lunch at Harvey Nics and the wealthy financiers of St Andrew Square, but there's no denying it has an extravagantly glamorous style. They bill themselves as the eighth trendiest hotel in the UK – and they have certainly made an effort in stylist points. The en-suite bathrooms have rainforest showers, and each bedroom has been designed on the theme of a different city – Paris (pink and baroque) New York (with brick walls, like a Greenwich village loft) Los Angeles (images of celebrities, breezy white and exposed stone décor) Atlantis (a fish tank and water wall). There are also several bars and a restaurant all decorated in an over the top and excessive style.

Middle range

Tiger Lily
125 George Street, 0131 225 5005, info@tigerlilyedinburgh.co.uk
www.tigerlilyedinburgh.co.uk
A gorgeously styled 4 star boutique hotel, Tiger Lily is on George Street, known as the 'style' street of Edinburgh. The décor incorporates intricate wallpaper and fabrics, stripped floorboards and wood-printed doors, and each one of the 33 rooms has an individual look, from candy pink decor, a 'black' room and wonderfully ornate Georgian suite with its contemporary four poster bed. Toiletries are provided by The White Company, there's a pre-loaded iPod in each room and the restaurant and bar are similarly ultra chic.

Angels Share

11 Hope Street, 0131 247 7000

www.angelsharehotel.com

What was formerly the Hudson Hotel has been given an ethereal name-change and a shiny makeover. Each room has the name of a Scottish musician or actor (for example Calvin Harris, Ewan McGregor, Emeli Sandi), and their picture on the wall, above large comfortable beds. While they have all the features you'd expect, some of the rooms are a little small, and their bar directly below can get quite noisy. It's in a great location in the West End, and in the morning the bar becomes a stylish place for breakfast and reading the papers.

Hotel Indigo

51 – 59 York Place, 0131 556 5577, reservations@hiedinburgh.co.uk

www.hotelindigoedinburgh.co.uk

In a very convenient spot near Broughton Street, Hotel Indigo is a style boutique in five combined townhouses with their original winding staircases and cornicing. There are 60 rooms with a vibrant colour scheme, luxury bathrooms with rainforest showers and 'media hub', and there's also a cocktail bar, restaurant and gym onsite.

Nira Caledonia

10 Gloucester Place, 0131 225 2720, info@niracaledonia.com

Niracaledonia.com

They claim to have a bohemian eclectic style, proudly without the tartan or the stuffed deer heads, and this boutique hotel is a place of luxury in a ritzy section of Edinburgh's New Town, near the embassies and cultural institutes, and just off one of the nicest streets in Edinburgh, quirky little Gloucester Lane. There is a choice of stately Georgian rooms and top of the range Jacuzzi suites of you want to 'splash' out. There's also a pleasant garden and courtyard at the back of this former residence of 19th century writer Christopher North.

Ricks Boutique Hotel

55A Frederick Street, 013 622 7800, info@ricksedinburgh.co.uk

www.ricksedinburgh.co.uk

Rick's is a boutique hotel and a cocktail bar, with ten rooms in a lime green and stripped wood colour scheme. The Hotel entrance is through the bar and restaurant, popular with the George Street crowd for afternoon and evening cocktails. The four star accommodation is comfortable, and while the rooms are quite small, they have all the features and luxuries, and a slight Japanese feel to the décor and corridors. The restaurant would also be great for an evening meal before heading out to experience some of the New Town bars nearby.

The Roxburghe hotel
38 Charlotte Square, 0871 423 4917
theroxburghe.com
Part of the Crowne Plaza group, the Roxburghe is a good choice for a central 4 star hotel, with stylish details, a location in a stately Charlotte Square mansion and their well regarded gym and spa facilities for all guests.

The George Hotel
19 – 21 George Street, 0131 225 1251, enquiries.thegeorge@principal-hayley.com
www.thegeorgehoteledinburgh.co.uk
The George Hotel is designed in a neo-classical style; dining rooms with leather seating, chandeliers and pillars, and with warm jewel toned rooms with the latest technology. This award-winning hotel is a haven of luxury that dates back to the 18th century, with Robert Burns and Walter Scott as rumoured former guests.

The Raddison Blu
80 High Street, 0131 557 9797
www.radissonblu.co.uk/hotel-edinburgh
Opened in 1989, the building was specifically built for the hotel in a top location in the Old Town, and designed to blend in with the character of the Royal Mile, although some would argue it wasn't so successful. The lobby and lounge has a monasterial feel to it with its arched corridors, and windows in the lounge look out onto Niddrie Street and Whistle Binkies pub – prime viewing to see what shenanigans are happening in the streets below.

The Dakota Hotel
11 Ferrymuir Retail Park, 0131 319 3690
www.dakotahotels.co.uk/hotels/edinburgh/
This weirdly futuristic black cube is just off the motorway before you get
to the Forth Road Bridge, and an interesting option if you are looking for
somewhere close to the airport. It may be mysterious on the outside, but once
you enter into it, there's an African feel to the décor, all browns and animal
prints, and the bar and restaurant are decked out like a warm New York grill.
The rooms are comfortable and good value with motifs that link it to the
Dakota plane theme.

Good value

Motel One
18 – 21 Market Street, 0131 220 0730, Edinburgh-royal@motel-one.com
www.motel-one.com
Motel One, a German chain of stylish hotels, is one of the newest hotels in
the city centre and the rooms are comfortable, the lounge area feels modern
and relaxing, and they do a good buffet breakfast as an extra for £7.50. With
a blue and beige colour scheme in the décor and on the staff, it does have the
slight feel of a budget airline, but rooms are from £69, and it's located right
by Waverley Station and below the Royal Mile.

The Grassmarket Hotel
94 – 96 Grassmarket, 0131 220 2299, grassmarket@centraledinburghho-
tels.co.uk
www.thegrassmarkethotel.co.uk
One of the best value hotels in the city centre, The Grassmarket Hotel is no
frills but comfortable, with slightly uneven, rickety floors and in an interesting old building. It's above Biddy Milligan's bar so the music can get a bit
load if you are on the lower floors.

Frederick House Hotel
42 frederick Street, 0131 226 1999, reservations@frederickhousehotel.com
www.frederickhousehotel.com

This 3 star hotel a couple of minutes walk from Princes Street is a good choice for exploring the New Town. The décor with its tartan curtains and bedspreads is fairly generic, but it's comfortable and the building is impressively grand and Georgian. There is no restaurant, but they include a complimentary breakfast from the Café Rouge across the street.

Fraser Suites
12 – 26 St Giles Street, 0131 221 7200, Edinburgh@fraserhospitality.com
Edinburgh.frasershospitality.com
In the site of old newspaper offices, these luxury but good value rooms and apartments have self-catering facilities, all modern features, Designers Guild fabric interiors (although rather beige) and a very central location opposite St Giles Cathedral on the Royal Mile. Some suites have living rooms, kitchens and their Broadsheet Café does breakfast for guests.

Bed and Breakfasts

Garlands Guesthouse
48 Pilrig Street, 0131 554 4205
Very near Leith Walk, and close to Pilrig Park, this guest house is friendly, relaxed and comfortable, with a plush Edinburgh townhouse feel to the decor, with a hot breakfast, including porridge, cooked up by the owner every morning.

Ardmor House
74 Pilrig Street, 0131 554 4944, info@ardmorhouse.com
www.ardmorhouse.com
Owned by a gay couple, and also welcoming of every sexual orientation, Ardmor is a four star boutique B & B, with chic interiors in the rooms and living space. It's located just off Leith Walk and owners Robin and Barry will give you their personal recommendations for what's good in the area.

Southside Guesthouse
8 Newington Road, 0131 668 4422
www.southsideguesthouse.co.uk
Located near the university, this B & B, run by a friendly, helpful couple, is stylishly homely, located in a Victorian terraced house with chequered floors, rich-coloured

walls, bookcases and paintings. They do a full Scottish breakfast, some rooms have grand four-poster beds and they provide all the comforts and more.

Apartments

The Chester Residence
6 – 9 Rothesay Place, 0131 226 2075
www.chester-residence.com
Award-winning five star apartments in a grand Georgian house, all decorated with stylish furnishings in chocolate, plum and slate colours with leather sofas, fireplaces, and ultra luxurious bathrooms with double sinks and televisions. There are 23 apartments in four town houses, graded from club to penthouse.

Stay Edinburgh City Apartments
217 High Street, 0131 220 1585, info@stayedinburghcity.co.uk
www.stayedinburghcity.co.uk
With their central office down a dark close off the Royal Mile, they offer 32 apartments in different locations in the Old Town, many with a good view off the Royal Mile. They mostly do two bed apartments, and several with four bedrooms, but they all come with big, modern kitchens, separate living rooms, and some bedrooms have ensuites.

The Knight Residence
12 Laurison Place, 0131 622 8120
www.theknightresidence.co.uk
Comfortable 5 star serviced apartments located in West Port, an area known as the Pubic Triangle, but very near the heart of the Old Town, and only a few minute's walk from lively Tollcross. Each apartment has all the facilities you could ask for, iPod docking stations, big screen TVs with movie channels, a fully equipped kitchen, which comes with a welcome basket, and soundproofed windows to cut out the noise from the bustling streets outside.

Hostels

Castle Rock Hostel
15 Johnston Terrace, 0131 225 9666, castlerock@macbackpackerstours.com

Castlerockedinburgh.com
A comfortable and sociable hostel lying beneath the castle. Dorms are airy and spacious and there are two kitchens, several lounges and relaxation rooms for fun times or reading, screenings of a Scottish movie daily and lots of activities such as a pub crawl arranged by the staff. It also takes advantage of its historic and location, decking out its cavernous rooms and staircases like a medieval castle.

The Hostel
3 Clifton Terrace, 0131 313 1031, info@edinburghcitycentrehostels.co.uk
www.edinburghcitycentrehostels.co.uk
With a minimalistic design, this hostel feels light and airy, rather than the stereotypical dark and dingy backpackers, although the bunk beds are packed in, and some of the attic rooms feel like a tight squeeze. There's a stark, well-equipped kitchen and a garden and decking area. It's located in a terraced house near Haymarket station, west of Princes Street, and so the airport bus goes directly past.

Edinburgh Central Hostel
9 Haddington Place, 0131 524 2090
edinburghcentral.org
Located on Leith Walk in a big old former Council building, these cheap digs run by the Scottish Youth Hostel association are simple but comfortable and well equipped. Because of its size it lacks the personal touch of more intimate backpackers, but it is painted with bright colours and has a licensed restaurant as well as kitchen and living space.

Smart City Hostels
50 Blackfriars Street, 0131 524 1989
Smartcityhostels.com
This large hostel is located down in the Cowgate, and is quite the party place. It has its own bar and restaurant, Bar 50, with a courtyard, cheap drinks and pool tables a major part of the experience. The hostel open 24 hours a day, has 132 rooms with en-suites, and they put on activities such as a pub crawl and open mic nights.

AREA GUIDES

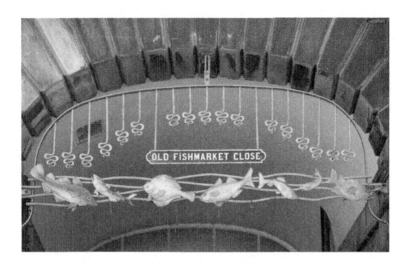

THE OLD TOWN

The Old town is the historical pulse of Edinburgh and absolutely thronging with visitors over the summer months. Having been built on different levels over centuries, with steep streets, narrow steps, dark closes and bridges, it's a place to explore and to get lost in.

The Royal Mile is Edinburgh's tourist centre, with its 'tartan tat' shops, traditional whisky bars and museums. Daniel Defoe called the Royal Mile "the largest, longest and finest street in the world." It stretches from The Castle all the way down to the Holyrood Palace, not quite a mile in distance but close enough.

It's a hodge-podge of different levels, closes, steps, steep hills and hidden gardens all intertwined. In medieval times, the classes would mix together but be confined to the different levels, living on top of one another – upper classes up top and away from the sewage, while the poor were confined to the smelly street level.

Sir William Brereton, a commander in Cromwell's army praised the "glory and beauty of this city" but inhabitants were "a most sluttish, nasty and slothful people."

It was a dirty, smelly city given the nickname Auld reeky. The Old Town was so overcrowded and built up, and with no sanitary health (people would chuck their waste out the window while crying 'gardy-loo') that it's no wonder a high percentage of the population were wiped out by bouts of plague in the 17th century.

Last century many of the older buildings were unfortunately knocked down and replaced by concrete 1960s monstrosities, which are now mixed in with buildings that date back to the 15th century.

The Cowgate, which runs below the Royal Mile, is an almost cavernous area of bars and clubs which can get rowdy at night. The area opens up as it approaches Holyrood Palace, Holyrood Park and the Scottish Parliament.

Things to see

Spend some time getting lost in the maze of steep, narrow closes, exploring the little gardens and sculptures hidden within this network of old stonework. Many of these closes also have interesting names – from Old Fishmarket Close to the gruesome sounding Fleshmarket Close.

Trunks Close is home of the Scottish Book Trust, with an interesting garland feature hanging down from the entrance. There's a nice circular garden with benches, a sculpture of a 'Cockalorum' and a statue of Geddes.

Trinity Àpse, a 15th century gothic kirk down Chalmers Close, is also home to the Brass Rubbing Centre, where you can create some artistic Celtic imagery.

The Mushroom Garden in Dunbar Close is a relaxing little retreat, originally created in the 19th century. Despite its name, it doesn't actually contain mushrooms – it was called this after the Mushroom Trust bequeathed the grounds to the city council to look after.

The Scottish Poetry Library, down Crichton Close, is a modern Scandinavian style building with wood and glass, which celebrates Scottish poetry through interactive exhibitions and an extensive collection.

The City Chambers is the official hub for the City of Edinburgh Council. In the courtyard on the left is the handprints of famous residents who have been given the Edinburgh Award – authors JK Rowling and Ian Rankin, Olympic cyclist Sir Chris Hoy and George Kerr, who taught karate to Mick Jagger.

On the right hand side of the courtyard are Annie Lennox's handprints, as part of a plaque to raise awareness of those living with HIV.

Another Royal Mile attraction is the world's most pierced women. She's a well-known character around town, but will quite rightly charge for a photo.

Gladstone's Land is a well-preserved 17th century town house, the only building with its original arcade front.

John Knox, minister of St Giles Cathedral, lived and died at John Knox House, a unique building down the High Street. He is buried in Parliament Square, beneath parking space no. 44.

The medieval Old Tollbooth was once the principal municipal building in the city, and was used for imprisonment and torture.

St Giles Cathedral, is gothic, arching, imposing, and in its courtyard contains The Heart of Midlothian. You may see people spitting down onto this cobble stone heart by St Giles Cathedral. It was a tradition for those who escaped the Old Tollbooth, originally at the front of the cathedral, to spit on it for luck. Football team Hearts get their name from this.

Canongate Kirk, the site of a Royal Wedding, was where Zara Phillips married Mike Tindall. The cemetery has views to Calton Hill and has the Canongate Mercat Cross which dates from 1128.

There's a legal graffiti site on New Street, where boards around a derelict piece of land have been painted by local graffiti artists.

Greyfriars Kirkyard is most famous as the resting place of Greyfriars Bobby, the little terrier that refused to leave his master's side, even after death, watching over his grave for 14 years. The little statue of Bobby is located at the top of Candlemaker Row.

Robots on the walls of Villager

Drinks

Halfway House
24 Fleshmarket Close, 0131 225 7101
www.halfwayhouse-edinburgh.com
Sunday to Wednesday 11am to 11.30pm, Thursday 11am to 12am, Friday
and Saturday 12.30pm to 1am
One of the smallest pubs in Edinburgh, tiny Halfway House gets its name
from being halfway down Fleshmarket Close, between Market Street and
Cockburn Street. It's intimate and friendly, with furnishings that look like
they have been around for many years, along with some of the locals. They
have a rotation of cask ales from all over Scotland, with a choice of four at
any one time, and the food is traditional Scottish with black boar sausages,
stoavies and oatcakes, Cullen skink and haggis, neeps and tatties.

Whiski Bar
119 High Street, 0131 556 3095, bar@whiskibar.co.uk
www.whiskibar.co.uk
Monday to Sunday 11am to 1am
Whiski is one of the best of the bars directly on the Royal Mile, recently
refurbished but keeping a traditional, cluttered feel. They have a large selection of whisky behind the bar, a good restaurant at the back, and in the
evenings the tables are pushed away for live Scottish music, where you are
welcome to join in with some singing or playing of guitar.

City Café
19 Blair Street, 0131 220 0125, info@thecitycafe.co.uk
www.thecitycafe.co.uk
Everyday 11am to 1am
City Cafe was *the* place to come pre-club for Edinburgh techno heads. It's still
a popular meeting point at the weekend for all sorts of characters, even if it
has been taken over by new management. Its art deco exterior now matches
its diner interior, with its Happy Days booths, juke box and soda counter.
You almost expect the staff to serve you on rollerskates. It has an extensive
burger list and an ice-cream counter, and later in the evening food gives

way to crowded evening drinks. Man v Food fans can also take part in the Ultimate Burger Challenge – eat it all and you get it for free (as well as a commemorative t-shirt for taking part.)

Bar Kohl
54 George IV Bridge, 0131 225 6939, info@barkohl.co.uk
www.barkohl.co.uk
Everyday 4.30pm to 1am
This funky bar specialising in infused vodka cocktails has been going since 1993 and was famed for their vodka importing expeditions to Russia. Kola cube infused Absolut vodka is one of the favourites, and they also do big pitchers to share such as a tribute to Fab ice-lollies. The cocktail menu is huge so there's sure to be a concoction for everyone. There's a hip-hop sound-track, burgers on the menu and space to dance.

Villager
49-50 George IV Bridge, 0131 226 2781
www.villagerbar.com/core/
Monday to Sunday 12pm to 1am
The Villager has the feel of a colonial lounge with potted palms, and gilded mirrors, but with colourful robot motifs on the wall. It's a cross between a bar and a restaurant, and because of this, seats can be hard to come by, unless you book ahead. Evenings become cocktail-fuelled raucous fun, with different DJs each week playing funky tunes.

Bristo Bar and Kitchen
41 Lothian Street, 0131 225 4186
www.bristo.co.uk
Monday to Saturday 11am to 1am, Sunday 12.30pm to 1am
Being a stone's throw from Edinburgh University, Bristo Bar and Kitchen goes for a bookish, student look with the leather sofas, wood-panneling and bookcase wallpaper. It's always been a popular place for student study meet-ups during the day, and for cocktails and food at nighttime, even in its previous incarnation as The Iguana.

CAROLINE YOUNG

The Holyrood 9a
9a Holyrood Road, 0131 556 5044
www.fullerthomson.com
Sunday to Thursday 9am to 12pm, Friday and Saturday 9am to 1am
With a trendy local crowd most nights, and local government workers doing Friday night drinks, Holyrood 9a is one of the more popular bars in this end of town. The burgers, with an inventive selection of toppings and served on chopping boards, are famous for being the tastiest in town. There are 11 beers on tap and a huge selection of Scottish bottled beers, as well as many craft beers from around the world.

The White Horse
266 Canongate, 0131 557 3512, thewhitehorsebar@hotmail.co.uk
Sunday to Thursday 12pm to 11pm, Friday and Saturday 12pm to 12am
With a long, illustrious history as a bar (Boswell and Johnston are believed to have met up here), the White Horse is surprisingly modern and cool. The back room is also a pleasant surprise – dark, candlelit, stone walls, comfy seats, and a screen for movies. It's also one of the only places to serve Glasgow's West beer on the east coast, and some good hearty food to go with the drinks.

BrewDog Edinburgh
143 Cowgate, 0131 220 6517, edinburghbar@brewdog.com
www.brewdog.com/bars/edinburgh
Monday to Saturday 12pm to 1am, Sunday 12.30pm to 1am
Microbreweries in Scotland are big right now, and the Brew Dog pub in the Cowgate is a real treat if you want to experiment with some different Scottish beers. The passionate beer-loving owners are renowned for pushing the boundaries with their stunts, from producing what they claimed was the world's strongest beer to serving freeze beer in stuffed dead animal bodies, and encouraging a fan to have the Brew Dog logo tattooed on his skin. Beers included Trashy Blonde, Punk IPA, 5am Saint and Alice Porter, which is flavoured with vanilla.

The Three Sisters

139 Cowgate, 0131 622 6801, the3sisters@g1group.com

www.thethreesistersbar.co.uk

Every day 9am to 1am

The Three Sisters is a popular but very average pub, which gets busy at the weekends and plays out to a soundtrack of cheesy chart music. But the old courtyard with a massive beer garden and benches is its big selling point. During the festival it's a good place to stop for an outdoor drink between shows, and it also acts as a venue for some free acts.

The Banshee Labyrinth

29-35 Niddry Street, 0131 558 8209, info@thebansheelabyrinth.com

www.thebansheelabyrinth.com

Everyday 12.30pm to 3am

They bill it as the most haunted place in Edinburgh – that's debatable, but its location in the old vaults is certainly unique. They also try to do everything in this place, as a bar, for food, with gigs and even a free cinema. They have a monthly zombie film club, host short film nights which celebrate local talent and there is a monthly comedy club.

Bannerman's Bar

212 Cowgate, 0131 556 3254

www.bannermanslive.co.uk

Monday to Saturday 12pm to 1am, Sunday 12.30pm to 1am

www.bannermanslive.co.uk

Bannerman's, one of the best known pubs down in the Cowgate, is a live music venue and 'rock and whisky bar' that has had some famous faces performing in their cellar-room venue, including an up-and-coming KT Tunstall. They also do a best of compilation CD, given out for free and featuring the highlights of their gigs over the past year, bringing some much welcomed support to bands starting out.

Angels with Bagpipes

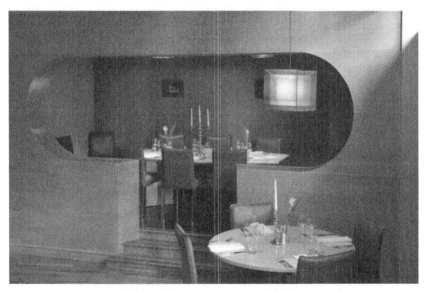

Michael Neave restaurant and kitchen

Restaurants

Monteiths
61 High Street, 0131 557 0330
www.monteithsrestaurant.co.uk
Monday to Friday 5pm to 12am, Saturday and Sunday 12pm to 12am
In Monteith Close under an enchanting tunnel of willow branches lit with fairy lights is Monteiths, a stylish yet seemingly secret restaurant. Inside is dark and cosy with tweed and tartan furnishings, mahogany and contemporary prints on the wall. They specialise in Scottish food, seafood and steaks and serve up cocktails from its backlit bar.

Angels with Bagpipes
343 High Street, 0131 220 1111
12pm to 10pm Monday to Sunday
www.angelswithbagpipes.co.uk
Described by its owners as being a restaurant where Rabbie Burns would take Sofia Loren on a date, Angels with Bagpipes is a sophisticated, romantic take on a Scottish tradition, as shown in their statue of a voluptuous angel holding some bagpipes (inspired by a statue of the Thistle Chapel of St Giles Cathedral). The menu features wildly inventive texture and taste combinations, Scottish meats and fish and some rich, exotic deserts.

The Outsider
15/16 George IV Bridge, 0131 226 3131
Monday to Sunday 12pm to 11pm
With a non-descript grey façade, an interior that uses the stripped, back to basics interior of wood, metal and glass, and a name possibly inspired by the Camus novel, The Outsider has worked to create that sense of a maverick in town. It became a destination restaurant after being raved about from its first day of opening. Food is well executed and there are great views of the castle from the back windows too.

La Cucina at Missoni
1 George IV Bridge, 0131 220 6666, info.edinburgh@hotelmissoni.com
Everyday 12.30pm to 3pm and 6pm to 11pm

CAROLINE YOUNG

www.hotelmissoni.com
With the obsessive design detail of the boutique hotel, Missoni's authentically Italian restaurant features the Missoni designed homeware in stylish monochrome, signature tablecloths and tapestry design on the wall. The food is stylish, modern Italian using the freshest ingredients, selected by Michelin star chef Giorgio Locatello.

Michael Neave Kitchen and Whisky Bar
21 Old Fishmarket Close, 0131 226 4747, reservations@michaelneave.co.uk
www.michaelneave.co.uk
Tuesday to Saturday 12pm to 2.30pm and 5.30pm to 10pm. Bar open until 12am. Closed Sunday and Monday.
One of the newest restaurants in Edinburgh, young chef Michael Neave's restaurant is located down one of the old closes in a vernacular building designed by Richard Murphy. Décor is clean, minimal, and Scandinavian and the food uses fine Scottish ingredients. The lunch menu is brilliant value – £7.95 for the express lunch of starter, main course with a choice of fish, red meat or vegetarian, and coffee with brownie and home-made ice-cream. A cost effective way to experience some Edinburgh fine-dining.

Wedgwood
267 Canongate, 0131 558 8737, info@wedgwoodtherestaurant.co.uk
Monday to Saturday 12pm to 3pm and 6pm to late, Sunday 12.30pm to 3pm and 6pm to late
www.wedgwoodtherestaurant.co.uk
A living room feel with muted striped walls, maroon lamps and white linen, Wedgwood is a refined fine-dining experience, and a little sanctuary off the Royal Mile, where diners are never rushed. The food by chef Paul Wedgwood is Scottish with a twist, and lunch is a very reasonable £16 for three courses, which change daily but could include tender rabbit with cauliflower croutons, pan-fried Coley with leaves the chef has foraged for himself, and banana, honey and vanilla cheesecake, all beautifully presented.

Empires
24 St Mary's Street, 0131 466 0100, reservations@empirescafe.co.uk
Empirescafe.wordpress.com

Monday to Thursday 5pm to 11pm, Friday to Sunday 12pm to 11pm

A Byzantium treat in the heart of the old town, Empires is decked out like a Kasbah with soft, low seating in the mezzanine, tables and booths on the ground floor and lots of Turkish artifacts in every nook and cranny. The Turkish food is offered tapas style – either selecting lots of dishes to share, or keeping your own choice of five to yourself, served on the one plate.

Vinyasa

34 St Marys Street, 0131 556 6776

www.vinyasaedinburgh.co.uk

Every day 12pm to 2pm, 5.30pm to late

A glitzy, colourful Indian restaurant as if from a Bollywood version of Mumbai, but serving traditional Bangladeshi and Indian food. Monday night is curry club and you can choose from a selection of authentic food such as cauliflower pakora, tender lamb on the bone, saag paneer and egg pudding or for desert. The a la carte menu is well-priced and well portioned, and with a lot of variety in the dishes from the North of India.

David Bann

56 -58 St Mary's Street, 0131 556 5888, info@davidbann.co.uk

www.davidbann.com

Monday to Friday 12am to late, Saturday and Sunday 11am to late

The vegetarian restaurant of Edinburgh, David Bann has an eclectic menu of dishes from around the world at reasonable prices. Starters and snacks include Thai broccoli fritters or olive polenta with roasted vegetables and goats curd, mains include mushroom strudel or chilli pancake with sweet potato and courgette and chocolate sauce, and a good selection of vegetarian wines, all served up in a warm, modern space.

Hanam's Restaurant

3 Johnstone Terrace, 0131 225 1329, hanams@hotmail.co.uk

Everyday 12pm until late

www.hanams.com

A Kurdish and Middle Eastern restaurant decked out in an authentic style with dark red walls, lots of embroidered Kurdish textiles and ceramics, and

Middle Eastern music on the stereo. Tables on the terrace at West Bow look out onto Victoria Street. The speciality is a variety of traditional shish kebabs that can be served Kurdish or Iranian style, and with rice dotted with pomegranate and dried berries, but you can also choose a selection of hot and cold mezze to share. They offer BYOB with no corkage charge.

The Secret Garden
Castlehill, 0131 225 5613
www.thewitchery.com
Part of iconic The Witchery, the Secret Garden is accessed through a narrow close and down some steps. It has a magically gothic feel to it, almost like a haunted conservatory with its candlesticks, chandeliers and foliage. French windows lead out onto an outdoor terrace. There's a two-course lunch for £15.95 and the menu features heavily with seafood, game such as Tweeddale pigeon breast, and locally sourced ingredients.

Coffee and cheap eats

Circus
8 St Mary's Street, 0131 556 6963
www.circusbistro.com
Monday to Sunday 8am to 1am
A treat of a café with a bohemian vibe and an outdoor courtyard enclosed by a stone wall, with carved wooden benches, hanging baskets and trellises, Circus makes a deserved break from the bustling Royal Mile. Owned by the Turkish family behind neighbouring Empires, they sell coffees, teas, Turkish snacks, soups, cakes and breakfasts that will set you up for the day.

The Baked Potato Shop
55 Cockburn Street, 0131 225 7572
Monday to Sunday 9am to 8pm
You ask for a small one, but somehow you still end up with one of the largest baked potatoes you've seen, served up with a choice of veggie fillings including haggis and chilli, with cheese and salads. A queue snakes out the bright

red door at lunchtime, and it's a bit of a squeeze with only one table in the shop, but take your tatty to go, and find a quiet outdoor perch.

Favorit

19 – 20 Teviot Place, 0131 220 6880

Monday to Thursday 12pm to 1am, Friday and Saturday 12pm to 3am, Sunday 12pm to 1am

Favorit is popular for weekend after-midnight munchies, a place that is one step up from the chippy and kebab shop. After 6pm you have to order drinks with your food, but they do reasonably priced burgers, quesadillas, pizza and other snacks that go well with a beer.

Caffe Lucano

37 – 39 George IV Bridge, 0131 225 6690

Monday to Friday 7am to 10pm, Saturday 8am to 10pm, Sunday 9am to 8pm

www.caffelucano.com

Caffe Lucano is a Scottish Italian family run café with a counter 'viennoiserie' filled with pastries, cakes and breads, crispy pizzas, healthy salads, inventive sandwiches and the smell of espresso in the air. The egg-based breakfasts are also a class above.

Hannah Zakari

Analogue Books

Shops

Royal Mile Whisky Trail
379 High Street, 0131 225 3383
www.royalmilewhiskytrail.com
Monday to Wednesday 10am to 6pm, Thursday to Saturday 10am to 8pm,
Sunday 11am to 6pm
One of the best places in the Old Town to buy whisky, from high-end
to more obscure. The staff are very helpful and knowledgeable, and will
give you tastings and can guide you to the type of whisky you may be
looking for. They also have a good selection of beers, wines and other
spirits.

Cranachan and Crowdie
263 Canongate, 0131 556 7194
www.cranachanandcrowdie.com
Tuesday to Sunday 11am to 6pm
A good place to stock up on the Scottish snacks, with oatcakes from Perthshire
and Aaron, Stoats porridge bars, Cream o' Galloway ice-cream served in a
cone, tablet and fudge and lots of other typically Scottish foods from all
over the country. Also look out for Puffin Poo, a particular treat from the
Shetlands, which sounds stranger than it is.

The Fudge House
197 Canongate, 0131 556 4172, info@fudgehouse.co.uk
fudgehouse.co.uk
The windows filled with mounds of different types of fudge could be
enough to lure you in, but they make all their own fudge on the premises.
With eight types of chocolate fudge, butter tablet and unusual twists
such as Lemon Meringue Pie and praline and Drambuie, all made by
a Scottish Italian family who have had their shop on the Royal Mile
since 1949.

Analogue Books

39 Candlemaker Row, 0131 220 0601, info@analoguebooks.co.uk

Monday to Saturday 10am to 5.30pm, Sunday 12pm to 4pm

http://www.analoguebooks.co.uk/

Analogue sells beautifully illustrated books, design magazines and illustrated zines by talented, up and coming artists and illustrators. Every item has been hand-selected, many are from local artists and there are also screen-prints, t-shirts and an exhibition space.

Old Town Context

42 – 44 Cockburn Street, 0131 629 0534, info@contextinteriors.co.uk

www.oldtowncontext.co.uk

Monday to Saturday 10am to 6pm, Sunday 11am to 5pm

If you are looking for a Scottish souvenir, but want to avoid the usual tartan tat, then this is the place to come. Illustrated cards of Ian Rankin, The Proclaimers, Sean 'Big Tam' Connery and the Forth Rail Bridge, 'You'll have had your trams' tea towels, the Edinburgh Zoo pandas – all the contemporary issues turned into tourist gifts.

Underground Solushn

9 Cockburn Street, 0131 226 2242, info@undergroundsolushn.com

Monday to Wednesday 10am to 6pm, Friday and Saturday 10am to 6pm, Thursday 10am to 7pm, Sunday 12pm to 6pm

www.undergroundsolushn.com

Edinburgh's only independent dance and electronic record shop which is a well-respected place to buy dance music vinyl. As well as new releases, old classics and collectables, they sell technology such as turntables mixers and speakers. You can also put on headphones and have a listen in store to new releases and old classics.

Whiplash Trash

53 Cockburn Street, 0131 226 1005

Whiplash Trash is the place to come piercings, kinky clothing and contraptions, and an entire wall devoted to bongs. It's been on Cockburn Street for years in various guises, but now specialises in legal highs and paraphernalia. They also sell hoodies, t-shirt and PVC.

The Frayed Hem

45 Cockburn Street, 0131 225 9851, thefrayedhem@hotmail.com

www.thefrayedhem.com

Monday to Saturday 10.30am to 5pm, Sunday 12pm to 5pm

The Frayed Hem is crammed with affordable vintage pieces, with bargain bins of ties and scarves, and racks of velvet jackets and vintage cycling jerseys. They also sell Cobra 83 custom made blazers waistcoats, and unique designs by Larissa Guzova.

Rene Walrus

30 St Marys Street 0131 558 8120, janet@renewalrus.co.uk

www.renewalrus.co.uk

Monday to Saturday 10am to 6pm, Thursday 11am to 7pm, Sunday appointment only

An accessory shop founded by an Edinburgh College of Art student, who designs and creates all the pieces in an Edinburgh workroom with her small team. They particularly specialise in wedding accessories but there are intricate 1920s style headdresses, glittering pendants and Art Deco style cuffs. Rene Walrus was nominated for a Scottish Fashion Award in 2012.

Hannah Zakari

43 Candlemaker Row, 0131 516 3264, enquiries@hannahzakari.co.uk

Tuesday to Saturday 11am to 5.30pm, closed Mondays

www.hannahzakari.co.uk

What began as an online shop selling kooky, quirky jewellery, clothing, interiors and stationary by independent designers, has become a boutique on Candlemaker Row. Owned by Rachael Lamb, she chose the name Hannah Zakeri to reflect her love of all things Japanese, and the cutesy artefacts certainly have a Harajuku feel.

Victoria Street, the Grassmarket and West Port

With its brightly painted shop fronts, cobbles and Upper Bow terrace walkway, Victoria Street is one of the most unique and coolest streets in Edinburgh's Old Town. It curves down into the Grassmarket from George IV Bridge and was originally constructed in the 18th Century as an access point from Grassmarket to Lawnmarket.

West Port and the intersection at Lady Lawson Street is also known as the 'pubic triangle' for the number of strip clubs and 'saunas' in the area. But it's also home of the Edinburgh College of Art, meaning that it's filled with plenty of stylish and arty looking students milling around, or hanging out in the nearby cafes and suitably musty independent bookshops. The Wee Red Bar, ECA's student union, is open to the public and has some good nights on, catering to indy and techno fans.

The Grassmarket once had a pretty rough reputation as a place for vagrants, but nowadays it is a rowdy, lively place on a Friday and Saturday night, particularly as a favourite for hen and stag parties doing pub crawls along the row of bars in the gabled historic buildings.

Despite being recently pedestrianised and with European-style pavement cafes, the Grassmarket still has this rough edge. It has a mix of social housing, hostels and private accommodation, which can lead to some frustration with the late nights and street noise, and an underlying problem of alcohol and drug issues.

Most of the buildings are from the 18th century, influenced by the Dutch gable design, but you can still see the Medieval history in the area.

From the 15th century right up to before the First World War The Grassmarket was a cattle market, lying conveniently below the castle crags. In medieval times, stables would have been set up to store and fatten the stock, before being butchered and sold at the Fleshmarket, up in the Old Town.

The Grassmarket was also famously a place for public executions around the Merkat Cross, where many unfortunates faced a public hanging, and for the stories of infamous body snatchers Burke and Hare.

Things to see

The Martyr's Cross marks the site of the public gallows where over 100 covenanters were hung.

The Bow Well was built in 1681 as the first source of piped running water, and was designed by Robert Milne. There's a carving of the Edinburgh coat of arms and the motto Nisi Dominus Frostra (without God, everything fails.)

The White Hart Inn is one of the oldest pubs in Edinburgh. Esteemed and infamous guests have included Wordsworth, mass murderers Burke and Hare and Robert Burns, who spent his last night in Edinburgh here in 1791.

10 West Bow is Major Weir's house, the sight of some mystical goings in the 17th century. Weir and his sister came to a grizzly end when they confessed to witchcraft and were executed for it. He became known as The Wizard of West Bow and the sounds of a 'spirited' party was said to come from their home even after their deaths.

The Grassmarket and its row of pubs

Under the Stairs

Drinks

The Beehive

18 – 20 Grassmarket, 0131 225 7171

www.taylor-walker.co.uk

Monday to Saturday 9am to 1am, Sunday 12.30am to 1am

While the Beehive is a run of the mill Grassmarket pub, its beer garden is one of the best kept secrets in the area. Located at the back of the pub, it has benches with umbrellas and heaters and a leafy multi-terrace level - a perfect place for enjoying an afternoon pint on a sunny day. The pub itself is cavernous and historical, with some secret rooms in the upstairs restaurant.

Under the Stairs

3a Merchant Street, 0131 466 8550, info@underthestairs.co.uk

Monday to Saturday 12pm to 1am, Sunday 12pm to 12am

This basement bar in the Old Town is a hipster's paradise, offering table service, for a civilised way to cut out the need for being crammed at the bar. The interior is shabby chic and eclectic, with odd pieces of furniture and lamps, a goldfish tank and changing artwork and photography on the wall. Try one of their seasonally inspired cocktails, or take a risk on the spice levels of a Chilli Palmer. It's a place for students, backpackers with style or young trendy types.

The Bow Bar
80 West Bow, Victoria Street, 0131 226 7667, thebowbaredinburgh@gmail.com
Monday to Thursday 12pm to 12am, Friday and Saturday 12am to 1pm, Sunday 12pm to 11pm
The Bow Bar is a classic, old-school pub in which conversation rules over TV and music. It doesn't go for the overly cluttered décor, and still has the original 1920s brass founts for their beers. It also offers a trip around Scotland with its 230 malts, and cask and bottled beers from around the country. The food is kept simple, providing pies and soup from neighbouring Grain Store restaurant.

Dragonfly
52 West Port, 0131 228 4543, info@dragonflycocktailbar.com
www.dragonflycocktailbar.com
Every day 4pm to 1am
Only a hop away from the Grassmarket, but a world away from its rugby and tourist bars, Dragonfly is an award-winning cocktail bar. Hip Hop on the decks, Kung Fu stencils on the wall, and bar decor that resembles old world colonial, it has an ironic sense of fun when it comes to cocktails. More manly options including that Scots classic A Half n a' Hoof (not for the faint hearted), Sage against the Machine, a Guinness Daiquiri and a Marty McFly 'Or Don't Call me Chicken'. (Told you they did hip irony well.)

The Blue Blazer
2 Spittal Street, 0131 229 5030, theblueblazer@live.co.uk
Monday to Saturday 11am to 1am, Sunday 12.30pm to 1am
The Blue Blazer is a traditional pub with two-rooms that get packed out at the weekends, selling a large selection of cask ales and whisky to a mixed crowd. It's popular with tourists, bearded students and performers during the festival, for its relaxed but rough around the edges atmosphere.

Restaurants

Grain Store
30 Victoria Street (1st floor), 0131 225 7635, contact@grainstore-restaurant.
co.uk
www.grainstore-restaurant.co.uk
Every day 12pm to 2pm and 6pm to 10pm
You enter this restaurant by going up the stairs and into an old stone room
with cosy little alcoves. The converted warehouse still has its original vault-
ing and archways and it really adds to the romantic setting, especially under
candlelight. They serve high quality Scottish meats and fish – scallops from
Orkney, lobster from the west coast, Scottish wood pigeon –local produce
such as wild leaves, mushrooms, beetroot, homemade bread and cheese from
local producers.

Viva Mexico
41 Cockburn Street, 0131 226 5145
www.viva-mexico.co.uk
Monday to Friday 12pm to 2pm, 6pm to 10.30pm
Saturday 12pm to 4.30pm, 4.30pm to 10.30pm, Sunday 6pm to 10pm
Run by the Gonzalez family, Viva Mexico is Edinburgh's original Mexican
restaurant, done up with bright paints, striped cloth, sombreros and cactus
decorations. The restaurant is split over two floors and with little alcoves,
and the food is fresh, zesty but filling. Burritos, enchiladas, tostadas and
chimichanga are served with rice, refried beans, guacamole, sour cream and
jalapenos, with smaller portions for lunchtime. If you have room for desert,
then try the homemade chocolate chilli cheesecake.

Timberyard
10 Lady Lawson Street, 0131 221 1222
www.timberyard.co
Tuesday to Saturday 12pm to 1.30pm and 5.30pm to 9.30pm, closed Sunday
and Monday
Timberyard is a family run business located in a converted 19th Century warehouse that was once home to Lawson's Timber. It's a restaurant that goes back

to basics with its butchery and smokehouse, fresh produce grown on site, an outside seating area and a stone outhouse that can be booked for groups of up to ten. As well as local produce, they stock craft beers like William Brothers and Black Isle and cocktails made from their own syrups and infusions.

Hula Juice Bar

Love Crumbs

Coffee and cheap eats

Oink

34 Victoria Street, 07771 968 233, info@reiver-foods.co.uk

www.oinkhogroast.co.uk

Every day 11am to 6pm

With a whole roasted pig sitting in the window, Oink does exactly what it says on the tin. Serving up finger-licking Scottish roast hog bred in the Borders. You buy the succulent meat sliced and served in a roll, with an option of apple sauce, chilli, cheese and even haggis. Snap up one of the few tables inside, or have your roll to eat on the move. They even provide whole roast hogs for private parties, which can serve up to 500.

Hula Juice Bar

103-105 West Bow, 07877 453 375, hello@hulajuicebar.co.uk

Every day 8am to 6pm

www.hulajuicebar.co.uk

With a bright and kitsch tropical interior of colourful chairs, frangipani prints and mini-palms, Hula Juice brings a taste of Hawaii to Edinburgh. As one of the few juice and smoothie bars in the city, they do fruit concoctions to sit or take-away, as well as salads, soups and paninis. They can also do three to five day juice cleanses if you are feeling in need of a detox. And if that's not enough reason to visit, it was also voted best Edinburgh café 2013 by readers of local magazine The Skinny.

Love Crumbs

155 West Port, 0131 629 0626, yoohoo@lovecrumbs.co.uk

www.lovecrumbs.co.uk

Monday to Friday 10.30am to 7pm, Saturday 10.30pm to 6pm, Sunday 12pm to 6pm

A bakery next to a strip joint and a vintage store – you can't get more retro than that. The lady bakers of love crumbs can custom make your cakes if your order in advance. So either pop by for a treat, or order your brownies how you want them – with or without nuts, soured cherries or made vegan. It has an artist's workroom feel with distressed floorboards, a piano that can be used as a table, and cakes displayed in an antique bureau. There are baskets of huge meringue, a lavender and blackcurrent Victoria Sponge and plenty of scones. It's popular with art students from the Edinburgh College of Art, across the road.

Armstrongs Vintage Emporium

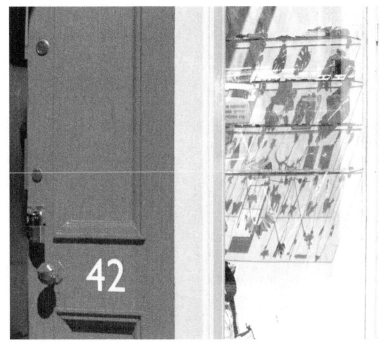

Red Door Gallery

Shops

Walker Slater

46 and 20 Victoria Street, 0131 220 2636

www.walkerslater.com/edinburgh

Monday to Wednesday and Friday 10am to 6pm, Thursday 10am to 6pm, Saturday 10am to 5pm, Sunday 11am to 5pm

If you want to stock up on Scottish tweed, Walker Slater is the place to come. Menswear is at number 20 and ladies-wear is further down the hill at 46. Started in the Highlands, the company do made to measure tailoring, funky tweed satchels, stylish coats and tweed skirts. The ladies shop is worth visiting to see the interior - winding stone steps leading up to the second floor and little alcoves. But because of the high quality of the tweed, items don't come cheap – expect to pay £300 for a coat.

Swish

22-24 Victoria Street, 0131 225 7180

www.swishlife.co.uk

Monday to Sunday 11am to 5pm
Colourful and kooky clothing from brands sourced from around the world, including Yummi, Vero Moda, Bellfield and American Apparell. They also sell men's clothing and skatewear and have a T-shirt store at 50 Cockburn Street.

Demijohn
32 Victoria Street, 0131 225 4090
www.demijohn.co.uk
Monday to Saturday 10am to 6pm, Sunday 11.30am to 5pm
Demijohn calls itself a liquid deli, and it's a paradise of liqueurs, oils, vinegars, whisky and gins. The barrels of liquid can be decanted into a variety of types and sizes of glass bottles, sealed with a cork, and with the option of having a personalised message marked onto the bottle. Some of the treats made by Demijohn include Sloe gin, ginger wine, chocolate orange crème liquor, and as well as Extra Virgin Olive oil, you could also keep it local with Perthshire rapeseed oil.

The Red Door Gallery
42 Victoria Street, Edinburgh, 0131 477 3255
Monday to Friday 10.30am to 5.30pm, Saturday 10.00am to 6pm, Sunday 11am to 5pm
www.edinburghart.com
As well as changing exhibitions of artwork, the Red Door Gallery sells artisan gifts by Scottish artists, including prints, jewellery, record-sleeve and ginger-haired people colouring books, cushions and funny little make-your-own gifts of paper animals, Battersea power station and tea towels that be converted into a sewing project.

K1 Yarns Knitting boutique
89 West Bow, 0131 226 7472
www.k1yarns.co.uk
Monday to Thursday 11am to 6pm, Friday 11am to 4pm, Saturday 11am to 5pm, Sunday 11am to 5pm

With knitting having a resurgence amongst young people, K1 Yarns provides high quality Scottish yarns as well as fair-trade handmade yarns from Uruguay and Alpaca. They can also offer good advice for beginners and if you fancy some chill-out knitting time, they have some comfy chairs where you can clack away with the knitting needles. They do beginners classes in crocket and knitting on a Sunday.

Golden Hare
102 West Bow, 0131 629 1396
Goldenharebooks.com
Every day 10am to 6pm
With displays of beautifully wrapped books in the window, and a hand-selected range of fiction, poetry and illustrated books, Golden Hare is a lovely bookshop to spend some time. You can also choose a record to play while you browse through the books and they have changing artwork on the walls.

Armstrongs Vintage Emporium
www.armstrongsvintage.co.uk
83 The Grassmarket, 0131 220 5557, info@armstrongsvintage.co.uk
Monday to Thursday 10am to 5.30pm, Friday and Saturday 10am to 6pm, Sunday 12pm to 6pm
With its musty, second hand smell and ceiling high racks of clothes, Armstrongs is a treasure trove of second hand delights. Friendly staff will help you pull down items from the top reaches of the shop, and it's all arranged by type – kilts, wedding dresses, tweed jackets, leather trench coats, old Levis, and boxes full of cravats, ties and hats. The shop was established in 1840 and its long been seen as the iconic place to come for vintage. There are also smaller branches at 64 – 66 Clerk Street and 14 Teviot Place.

Cookie
29a Cockburn Street, 0131 622 7260, pieintheskyltd@hotmail.com
Monday to Saturday 9.30am to 6pm, Sunday 12pm to 5pm
Cookie has an excellent selection of colourful printed dresses in all sorts of shapes and styles. In fact, they possibly stock the best selection of frocks in

the city and it's a real dress-lovers paradise. Peter Pan collars, polka dots, flower prints, sailor-style, and some boy's bomber jackets.

Burke and Hare

There was never a more revered duo than William Burke and William Hare – bodysnatchers, mass murderers and profiteers who terrorised Edinburgh in the early 19th Century.

Burk and Hare, two Irish immigrants who worked out there was a good profit in killing and selling the bodies to medical science, first met at Log's Lodgings in Tanner's Close, West Port. It was a lodging house run by William and Hare and girlfriend Margaret Laird, where Burke moved into with his girlfriend Helen McDougal.

They murdered residents at the lodgings and anyone else who they thought wouldn't be missed. Prostitute Mary Halden was lured to and killed at Log's Lodgings, as was her daughter Peggy, after she came looking for her mother. Teenage prostitute Mary Paterson was murdered in Burke's brother's house in Gibb's Close in the Cannongate.

A famous victim was Daft Jamie, a children's entertainer. Because he was such a popular character, students at the anatomy class recognised him and started to get suspicious.

Burke and Hare fell out as they got greedy, and Burke and Helen were arrested for their part in the murder of Mary Docherty, whose body was discovered in the lodgings. Because of the lack of evidence, Hare turned informant, meaning he got off the hook while Burke was hung in the Lawnmarket. He was executed on January 28 1829 in front of a huge crowd, and then given to students for dissecting. His skin was used by students to bind a book, stamped in gold with 'Burke's skin 1829'. This book, and Burke's death mask, is on display Surgeon's Hall Museum

Window display of the Cumberland Bar

NEW TOWN

The New Town covers the city centre areas of Princes Street, George Street, North to Cannonmills and west to Haymarket.

The New Town is Edinburgh's equivalent to Sloane or Knightsbridge; a residential area of expensive Georgian homes with bars, cafes and restaurants nestled beneath. It's a lived-in place full of interesting people and for bohemians, writers and artists to be inspired.

It was planned out in the 18th century as a way of easing the overcrowded slums of the Old Town. Its Georgian buildings still beautifully preserved and with crescent streets, cobbles, original oil lamps, leafy private gardens and boulevards.

It's an ideal place for a lazy afternoon wander. The type of place with hidden secrets beneath the picturesque exterior, a place you can get lost in exploring the boulevards and cobbled side streets, discover a quiet pub for an afternoon pint, or browse the art galleries and junk shops of Dundas Street. It's also magical at nighttime – the streetlamps give it a romantic glow, a Dickensian quality, and reflect in the damp cobbles after a rain shower.

The New Town was perfectly captured in the opening of Danny Boyle's Shallow Grave (1994), as the camera races through the cobbled streets and curved crescents, giving the area an edge.

The opening line may have been 'this could be any city, they're all the same', but like Trainspotting, the film defined Edinburgh in the 1990s, showing those cavernous, high ceilinged Edinburgh flats and their twisted staircases, home to students, wealthy eccentrics and yuppies alike.

The coolest streets to explore in the New Town are William Street with its pubs, Thistle Street with its little boutique shops, and funky Broughton

Street, but Dundas Street has a ton of art galleries, and Howe Street, leading down to Stockbridge has some good bars and cafés.

Princes Street is the main shopping street, lying in the shadows of Edinburgh Castle, its imposing fortress watching over the city. This is where all the usual high street shops can be found – Top Shop, Urban Outfitters, Primark and of course Edinburgh's own Harrods, Jenners.

Some people love George Street, some try to stay away. It's the street of sophisticates, the nouveau riche who park their Mercs on the centre-street parking, and the Friday night after-works drinks crew, still in their shirts and ties. George Street is topped and tailed by St Andrew Square, the location of Scotland's only Harvey Nichols, and exclusive Charlotte Square, home of the book festival every August.

The bars that populate George Street attract a dressed-up, young and coatless crowd looking for cocktails and designer beers. The best are The Living Room, Candy, Tiger Lily with its basement nightclub Lulu and the Opal Lounge, which has a door charge after 11pm. But there are also two Weatherspoon pubs, the Standing Order and Graham Bell, for cheap drinks if you don't mind the carpeted, airport lounge surroundings.

The Assembly Rooms, one of the main venues for the Edinburgh International Festival, was recently refurbished to preserve the heritage of the building and introducing Jamie Oliver's Jamie's Italian restaurant.

Thistle Street is a quiet street with independent clothes boutiques, for getting away from the usual high street shops on Princes Street.

"Only arseholes, wankers and tourists set fit in Rose Street," wrote Irvine Welsh in Trainspotting. That was in the 1980s, and some things have progressed since then, including the quality of the bars. But Thistle Street, only a few minutes walk from George Street has a far more relaxed vibe.

Tiger Lily

The Cumberland Bar

Photo courtesy of Bramble

CAROLINE YOUNG

Drinks

TigerLily
125 George Street, 0131 225 5005, info@tigerlilyedinburgh.co.uk
www.tigerlilyedinburgh.co.uk
Every day 8am to 1am
Tiger Lily's lounge and restaurant is a Hugh Hefner boudoir of purple velvet sofas, red lights, iridescent mosaic, pink flowers and wicker - and yet somehow it all seems to work. Their soundtrack transports you to an Ibiza terrace, they do half price cocktails on weekday evenings and the food menu is Asian fusion. They can also do an 'interactive' cocktail trolley where a mixologist can shake up cocktails directly at the table. It's a favourite of the style bunnies of George Street and the staff are friendly and attentive.

Tonic
34A North Castle Street, 0131 225 6431 info@bar-tonic.co.uk
www.bar-tonic.co.uk
Monday to Wednesday 5pm to 1am, Thursday 4pm to 1am, Friday 2.30pm to 1am, Saturday 1pm to 1am, Sunday 2.30pm to 1am
A romantic looking haven when the sun goes down, with its veil of fairylights beckoning people into the basement location, Tonic is a funky Manhattan-style bar, with an extensive list of cocktails, live acoustic music on a Thursday and a rotation of DJs over the weekend playing house and electronica.

Candy Bar
113 – 115 George Street, 0131 225 9179, info@candybaredinburgh.co.uk
www.candybaredinburgh.co.uk
Every day 12pm to 1am
A young and beautified Edinburgh crowd pours into this basement bar with its leather booths, its pumping music reverberating through the windows and an extensive list of cocktails and pitchers. There are DJs at the weekend and people spill out the door and onto the courtyard for smoking and chatting. They serve food until 7pm at the weekends, but you might find the music gets a little loud to hear the conversation over dinner. It's the kind of place a Made in Chelsea star may pop in for a guest appearance.

Soba

104 Hanover Street, 0131 225 6220, info@barsoba.co.uk

www.barsoba.co.uk

Monday to Saturday 12pm to 1am, Sunday 12.30pm to 1am

The popular Glasgow West End Pan-Asian restaurant and bar comes to Edinburgh with servings of Asian street food, and sharp cocktails. The décor is Tokyo and Bangkok graffiti, with long communal benches to eat at in the downstairs restaurant, and the main bar on the ground floor. The menu is a mix of Indonesian, Thai, Korean, Japanese, and Indian and there's an express two-course lunch menu for £9.95, but in the evenings the bar throbs with a bustling crowd and DJs play funk, soul and hip hop.

99 Hanover Street Bar

99 Hanover Street, 0131 225 8200

www.99hanoverstreet.com

Monday to Thursday 4pm to 1am, Friday 3pm to 1am, Saturday 12pm to 1am, Sunday 5pm to 1am

It has the kind of eclectic interior that could be a New York lounge or a 1940s piano bar, with dark wood, potted plants, chandeliers and sofas. But don't expect a quiet drink, it prides itself on seven days of events, from top DJs playing as a pre-club warm-up to cheap student nights on a Monday night, it's moved away from being an after-works drinking place to hosting some of the Edinburgh's players of the club scene.

The Black Cat Bar

168 Rose Street, 0131 225 3349, blackcatedinburgh@hotmail.com

theblackcatbar.com

Every day 11am to 1am

One of the best bars on Rose Street, the Black Cat are specialise in whisky and craft beers, with Black Isle beer on tap. They have Scottish live bands playing on Monday and Wednesday evenings and also encourage folk musicians to join in jamming sessions around the table. It's a darkly atmospheric place with a good, friendly vibe and some expert knowledge for recommend whisky.

The Guildford Arms

1 West Register Street, 0131 556 4312, guildfordarms@dmstewart.com

www.guildfordarms.com

Monday to Thursday 11am to 11pm, Friday and Saturday 11am to 12pm, Sunday 12.30pm to 11pm.

A very traditional boozer with real ale on tap, The Guildford Arms still has the original Victorian features – a Mahogany bar, ornate, high ceiling, a mezzanine with balcony, round tables and leather seats. It can get very busy in the evenings, with a lively atmosphere of people gathered around the bar for a pint.

Bramble Bar

16 A Queen Street, 0131 226 6343

www.bramblebar.co.uk

Every day 4pm to 1am

The people at Brambles really know their cocktails, mixing them up in a dark cavern under a tailors shop. It's the feeling of being part of a secret club that makes it special. Wile away an evening under candlelight and on cushioned Kasbah style seating and little alcoves, sipping on an Exile on Queen Street (cognac, Jagermeister, whole egg and salted caramel) or a lemony Miss Moffet, served in a teacup. Live DJs play soul and hip hop every weekend, to a full house.

Bon Vivant

51 Thistle Street, 0131 225 6055, info@bonvivantedinburgh.co.uk

www.bonvivantedinburgh.co.uk

Monday to Sunday 12pm to 1am

With a name that suggests a person who knows how to live the good life, Bon Vivant is an elegant, candlelit bar that is perfect for dinner, or some drink sophistication. With a regularly updated wine list and with carafes also on offer, a changing cocktail menu, and an eclectic selection of beers and ciders, they aims to cater for everyone, although it heads towards the high end with its prices and table service. They even have a wine panel of experts and locals to update their list, which includes a choice of over 30. Starters and Deserts

90

are offered in £1 samples so you can really try a bit of everything. Choice is definitely the word here.

The Cambridge Bar
20 Young Street, 0131 226 2120
www.thecambridgebar.co.uk
Sunday to Wednesday 12pm to 11pm, Thursday 12pm to 12am, Friday and Saturday 12pm to 1am
The Cambridge, with specialist Scottish beers on tap (William Brothers lager, Black Isle blonde and goldeneye) and popular for its menu of burgers, is a haven of relaxed coolness in a quiet spot only a few minutes from George Street. Special burgers include a Juicy Lucy with a choice of cheese melted inside a beef patty. Milkshakes are made with Mackie's ice cream, and add a shot of Myers rum for a Mia Wallace $5 shake experience.

The Oxford Bar
8 Young Street, 0131 539 7119
www.oxfordbar.co.uk
Monday to Saturday 11am to 12am, Sunday 12.30pm to 11pm
This is where Ian Rankin's detective John Rebus would come in for a swift pint between shifts. It's a no frills pub with a mix of clientele, close to the city centre but hidden away. The perfect, anonymous pub for a grizzled detective. The Ox even prides itself on its curmudgeonly bar staff, serving up the IPA to Rankin fans and locals alike. It also has a history of being a haunt for writers and artists, being in the midst of creative New Town.

The Voodoo Rooms
19a West Register Street, 0131 556 7060, info@thevoodoorooms.com
Thevoodoorooms.com
Monday to Thursday 4pm to 1am, Friday to Sunday 12pm to 1am
The Voodoo Rooms does sexy, opulent cocktail lounge with a side order of live music venue. It's the place to come to catch up and coming and established bands, and it also hosts comedy events during the festival. With the ornate, original features enhanced and elaborated upon (gilded cornices, curved leather booths, chandeliers), it's an upmarket space featuring a crowd

who are up for being seen, as well as those who want to catch up with their friends for a drink or two.

The Regent Bar

2 Montrose Terrace, 0131 661 8198, info@theregentbar.co.uk
www.theregentbar.co.uk
Monday to Saturday 12pm to 1am, Sunday 12.30pm to 1am
Between Easter Road and Calton Hill, the Regent Bar is Edinburgh's "gay real ale pub". However it doesn't stereotype itself as a gay pub and instead has a crowd of regulars who come in for the beers, a game of darts and some pub food. The bar also looks fairly traditional, but with a bizarre décor of tartan carpets, orange and red walls and leather sofas.

Star Bar

1 Northumberland Place, 0131 539 8070
www.starbar.org.uk
Monday to Saturday 11am to 12am, Friday 11am to 1am, Sunday 12.30pm to 12am
This gem of a little pub is hidden amidst the Georgian houses of the New Town, right at the end of Northumberland Place. While it serves standard pub drinks, it's got a foosball table, dart board and two juke boxes, and a small outdoor area with benches. It's a bustling place, with a friendly atmosphere from the students and artistic types who come in for a pint or an extended evening out.

The Cumberland

1 Cumberland Place, 0131 558 3134
www.cumberlandbar.co.uk
Monday to Saturday 11am to 1am, Sunday 12.30pm to 1am
When the sun comes out, the Cumberland's leafy beer garden, down a set of stony steps, is heaving with after-workers and New Town residents. There's a good selection of cask ales on tap and featured guest beers from small breweries, and while there's no music, there's plenty of chatter from the interesting characters who make it their local.

Kay's Bar
39 Jamaica Street, 0131 225 1858
www.kaysbar.co.uk
Monday to Thursday 11am to 12am, Friday 11am to 1am, Sunday 12.30am
to 11pm
Located down a cobbled lane, this tiny Victorian pub in a converted Georgian
coach-house is how you would imagine an old-fashioned pub to be, with its
plum-coloured interior, wooden panelling and coal fire. Conversations flow
among the bar staff and patrons, and they serve up real ales and pub grub. A
visit to Kay's Bar is like stepping into a slice of perfectly preserved history,
and a great retreat from the hub-bub of the city centre.

St Vincent Bar
11 St Vincent Street, 0131 225 7447
www.stvincentbar.com
Monday to Saturday 11am to 1am, Sunday 12.30pm to 1am
A pub that could be straight out of an Alexander McCall Smith novel, the
Vinnie is a small, cosy pub in the basement of a New Town tenement, painted
green and with a gas lamp out front. It has a loyal band of locals, an intimate
atmosphere around the bar, and seats outside to watch the world go by. It's a
good place to start at on the way up the hill into town.

Photo courtesy of The Dogs

Restaurants

Iglu

2B Jamaica Street, 0131 476 5333, mail@theiglu.com

www.theiglu.com

Tuesday to Thursday 4pm to 12am, Friday and Saturday 12pm to 1am, Sunday 12pm to 11am, Closed Monday

Iglu is a trendy little bar and restaurant that also does sustainable Scottish food very well, choosing local producers and organic where possible. There's a taste of Scotland six course menu that lets you explore many Scottish treats. It was one of the first places to offer Black Isle organic ale on tap. Look out for their slow food and whisky tasting events, which serves up Scottish food to compliment the whisky on offer.

Café Andaluz

77b George Street, 0131 220 9980

www.cafeandaluz.com

Monday to Saturday 12pm to 10pm, Sunday 12.30pm to 10pm

With an Antoni Gaudi inspired interior of white walls, mosaic, embroidered cushions, mirrors and Spanish carved wood, it's like stepping into some warm Mediterranean haven. You can choose a selection of tapas to share – cured meats, Spanish tortilla, and patatas bravas – making it a great little retreat from shopping or exploring.

Chaophraya

33 Castle Street, 0131 226 7614, Edinburgh@chaophraya.co.uk

www.chaophraya.co.uk

Monday to Saturday 11am to 10.30pm, Sunday 12pm to 10pm

One of Edinburgh's newest Thai restaurants, it's a glitzy, extravagant place with water features, lights, statues of Buddha and huge glass windows which offer a clear view of the castle. The menu offers Thai favourites as well as specialties including a refreshing green papaya salad and crispy pork belly with chilli. You could also have a drink before or after dinner in the glamorous sounding Palm Sugar bar.

Fishers in the City
58 Thistle Street, 0131 225 5109, city@fishersrestaurantgroup.co.uk
www.fishersbistros.co.uk
Everyday 12pm to late
"So fresh it will pinch your bum and call you darling" – that's what their sign used to say, anyway. Fishers does fine seafood in the city centre, serving up a consistently good seafood menu in smart surroundings, and with a fine selection of wine. It's a good place to come for champagne and oysters, or a big plate of fish and chips, served with peas and tartare sauce.

Dusit
49A Thistle Street, 0131 220 6846
www.dusit.co.uk
Monday to Saturday 12pm to 3pm, 6pm to 11pm, closed Sunday
Contemporary Thai food in a traditional setting with the stone walls, statues of Buddha and pieces of artwork by Bangkok students. It's a popular place, often busy during the week, with a menu of fresh, fragrant dishes that feel healthy - steamed vegetables in an oyster sauce, Thai soups that are said to boost the immune system, scallops and king prawns with garlic, chilli, lime and coriander, and the house special crispy duck.

Café St Honore
34 North West Thistle Street Lane, 0131 226 2211, eat@cafesthonore.com
www.cafesthonore.com
Café St Honore is an authentically French brasserie that always receives consistently good reviews. The checked floorboards, white linen table cloths and mirrored walls add to the Parisian atmosphere and the menu features Scottish/French twists with smoked mackerel pate with oatcakes, organic coq au vin and crème brulee served with shortbread.

The Dogs
110 Hanover Street, 0131 220 1208, info@thedogsonline.co.uk
www.thedogsonline.co.uk
Monday to Sunday 12pm to 10pm

Good value but high quality dishes with Scottish influence – fish kedgeree, haggis with black pudding and duck egg, devilled ox liver, and apple, short-bread and vanilla rice pudding. The space, with its white walls, benches, wooden chairs and dog motifs emblazoned on the walls and cushions, is relaxed and informal. It's a firm Edinburgh favourite which spawned some short-lived spin-offs, but this original is still going strong, particularly popular with a young crowd.

The Roamin' Nose
14 Eyre Place, 0131 629 3135, knock-knock@theroaminnose.com
www.theroaminnose.com
Tuesday to Friday 8.30am to 10pm, Saturday 10am to 10pm, Sunday 10am to 8pm, closed Monday
In a quiet position near King George V Park, The Roamin' Nose specialises in Mediterranean food served within a simple interior of white walls and brickwork. Good value pasta, salads and gnocchi are given a splash of special Etruscan olive oil imported by the chef, and served with glasses of prosecco. And they also do good value cooked breakfasts. There are jars of locally made marshmallows from the Marshmallow Lady, whose shop is nearby, and home-made cakes up on the counter.

Leo's Beanery

Cuckoo's Bakery

Cafes and cheap eats

Eteaket
41 Frederick Street, 0131 226 2982, hello@eteaket.co.uk
www.eteaket.co.uk
Monday to Saturday 9am to 6pm, Sunday 11am to 6pm
Is it tea you are looking for? Edinburgh's experts in leaf tea, Eteaket is on a mission to make tea sexy, sourcing from all over Asia and meeting tea masters in their quest. Their tea house has bright blue tables and chairs, a smell of fruit tea as you enter, and shelves stacked high with their own tins of tea for sale. Having made a name for themselves, their product is stocked

in Michelin starred restaurants and hotels in the UK, and their tea has such names as Chocolate Abyss, Bollywood Dreams Chai, Gunpowder Deluxe and the award-winning Organic Silver Needle.

Henderson's of Edinburgh
94 Hanover Street, 0131 225 2131
www.hendersonsofedinburgh.co.uk
Restaurant: Monday to Saturday 8am to 10pm, open Sunday during August and December 11am to 4pm
Bistro: Sunday to Wednesday 12pm to 8.30pm, Thursday to Saturday 12pm to 9.30pm
Deli: Monday to Friday 8am to 7pm, Saturday 1am to 6pm, Sunday 11am to 5pm
Henderson's vegetarian restaurant is an Edinburgh institution, having been run by the Henderson family since the 1960s, when veggie food was seen to be for hippies or kranks. Queue up along the salad and hot food bar to try selections of wholesome salads or hearty vegetarian meals. The veggie haggis is worth a go, and arguably tastes better than the real thing, spicy bean burgers are a favourite and the chocolate mousse is also out of this world. The Bistro round the corner on Thistle Street does table service, and you can also pick up take-away foods, breads and other wholesome Henderson's products from the deli shop.

Leo's Beanery
23/4 Howe Street, 0131 556 8403
www.leosbeanery.co.uk
Tuesday to Friday 8.30am to 5pm, Saturday 9am to 5pm, Sunday 10am to 5pm
In a tenement basement, with a patio that catches the sun and the cellar doors, which are a feature of the New Town, this family run café is the perfect antidote to the Starbucks and Costa coffees in town. It's a popular hangout for the New Town denizen at the weekend, creating a little place of escape with its nicely cluttered interior of stripped wooden tables and chairs, old cookbooks to flick through, daily specials on the blackboard, and delicious homemade cakes and scones at the counter.

French Press
25a Dundas Street, 0131 556 4336
Frenchpresscoffeecompany.co.uk
Monday to Friday 8am to 6pm, Saturday to Sunday 9am to 5pm
French Press's unique selling point is that it is Edinburgh's first 'brew bar'. It offers coffee created in a variety of ways, from espresso, cafetiere, drip-brew, aeropress, or Japanese V60 ceramic filter. The interior was designed by owner Gail Thompson, and it also serves up designer sandwiches from Wedgwood, the Canongate restaurant.

Wellington Coffee
33a George Street, 0131 225 6854
Monday to Friday 7.30am to 6pm, Saturday 8.30am to 6pm, Sunday 9.30am to 6pm
The original place in Edinburgh for a coffee New Zealand style, with flat whites and long blacks on the menu, and grinding up the Square Mile beans. They also serve gigantic homemade scones and brownies. There is outdoor basement seating, and an interior of simple black and white checkered floorboards and stripped wood walls.

Cuckoo's Bakery
150 Dundas Street, 0131 556 6224, hello@cuckoosbakery.co.uk
www.cuckoosbakery.co.uk
Closed Monday, Tuesday to Thursday 10am to 5.30pm, Friday 10am to 6pm, Sunday 11am to 5pm
On a shabby section of Dundas Street, with closed down shops and their walls of peeling old posters, is pretty Cuckoo's Bakery. An airy, popular café with a 1950s style kitchen with purple and white tiles, and a centrepiece cabinet of inventive cupcakes which are baked at 3am every morning by a team of bakers. They also sell custom-made crockery with Edinburgh landmarks etched in blue.

Indie Chic on Broughton Street

Shopping

Princes Street is the main shopping street with typical high street brands including a Top Shop, a large Primark, Urban Outfitters and iconic Jenners.

Scotland's only Harvey Nicols is on St Andrew Square, and round the corner Multrees Walk is a pleasant pedestrian shopping area with shops including Louis Vutton, Kate Middleton favourite Reiss, Mulberry and Michael Kors.

Multrees Walk leads to tatty St James Centre, located within a 1960s eyesore given the dubious title of one of Britain's carbuncles.

Shops on George Street are the high-end of high street – there's no Chanel or Westwood, but there is Rox jewellers, Space NK, Anthropologie, Hollister and The White Stuff, which has taken advantage of the features of the old hardware store Greys.

But you'll find a number of good independent shops on cobbled Thistle Street and in the West End near Shandwick Place, in a section called the West End Village.

Jane Davidson

52 Thistle Street, 0131 225 3280, online@janedavidson.co.uk

www.janedavidson.co.uk

Monday to Wednesday, Friday and Saturday 9.30am - 6pm, Thursday 9.30am to 7pm, Sunday 12pm -5pm

Jane Davidson is the independent Edinburgh boutique for designer fashion. It was founded in 1969 as a swinging shop selling only British brands like Jean Muir and Ozzie Clark. They now stock designers including Victoria Beckham and Roland Mouret, Diane von Furstenberg, M Missoni and Temperley. It's a place of luxury that allows you to try some new styles in a relaxed setting, and is considered one of the best boutiques in Scotland.

Covet

20 Thistle Street, 0131 220 0026, sales@thoushaltcovet.com

Thoushaltcovet.com

Monday to Saturday 10am to 6pm (open 7pm on Thursday), closed Sunday

A designer accessory shop which has been nominated for a Scottish Fashion Award, Covet is a passion of two young friends, Anna and Blaise, who select the unique pieces that blend high street and high end fashion in a relaxed, boutique setting. Designs include sunglasses by Missoni, broaches by Tatty Devine, scarves and funky leather purses by Becksondergaard and earrings by Scottish designer Euan McWhirter.

Pam Jenkins
41 Thistle Street, 0131 225 3242, info@pamjenkins.co.uk
www.pamjenkins.co.uk
Monday to Saturday 10am to 5.30pm
A little shoe lover's paradise, with ladies shoes and accessories by designers including Christian Louboutin, Jimmy Choo, Pretty Ballerinas and Rupert Sanderson, all displayed in a nice living room feel, complete with mantelpiece. The prices are splurge not steel, but it's an escape from the more hectic shops on Princes Street.

Kakao By K
45 Thistle Street, 0131 226 3584, girls@kakao.co.uk
www.kakao.co.uk
Monday to Saturday 10am to 6pm, (open 7pm on Thursdays)
A Scandinavian fashion and designer boutique, with a name meaning hot chocolate in Danish, Kakao by K sells Scandi labels that are unique to Scotland. The shop has the stark lines you would expect from Scandinavia and their collection of dresses, knitwear, shirts and accessories is clean, simple and in often muted tones.

21st century kilts
48 Thistle Street, 07774 757 222, orders@21stcenturykilts.com
21stcenturykilts.com
Tuesday to Saturday 10am to 6pm (open until 7pm on Thursday), closed Sunday and Monday
Designer Howie Nicholsby custom-makes kilts with a twist – using leather, denim, camouflage and gilt to create a unique garment that can be worn casual or formal, to ceilidhs or to weddings, as is the Scottish tradition. He has a ready to wear line featuring kilts, sporrans and belts, or you can contact for a personalised appointment.

Belinda Robertson Cashmere

13a Dundee Street, 0131 557 8118

www.belindarobertson.co.uk

Monday to Friday 9.30am to 6pm, Saturday 10am to 6pm, Sunday 12pm to 5pm

With a sudden resurgence in Scottish fabrics, particularly on the back of Chanel's 2012 show at Linlithgow Palace, Belinda Robertson Cashmere is now re-positioning itself as one of the world's leading cashmere brands. You can visit the original store in Edinburgh for luxury cashmere knits made in the Borders.

Unicorn Antiques

65 Dundas Street, 0131 556 7176

Unicornantiques.co.uk

Monday to Saturday 10.30am to 6.30pm, Closed Sunday

The name might conjure up Victoria Wood's Acorn antiques, but it's a veritable jungle of junk. The junk isn't organized in any way, so it's exactly how you would imagine it to be – that old smell of antiques, and chaotic stacks of any type of object you may be looking for, such as old postcards, teapots and jewellery.

Restaurant L'Ptit Folie

West End

The West End is the area around Charlotte Square, up to Dean Village and heading out to Haymarket Station and Shandwick Place.

It's an area of grand Georgian terraced boulevards, some interesting architecture, including the mock Tudor house holding the restaurant La P'tite Folie, and a section known The West End village. This includes William Street, one of Edinburgh's funky little streets – a cobbled den of busy pubs and independent shops.

Charlotte Square's central garden is a private garden for residents, so can't be accessed by the public apart from when it's opened up for the Edinburgh International Book Festival in August. For three weeks it becomes a bookish hub for writers and literature lovers with a programme of talks and masterclasses by established writers. It's also a relaxing place to grab some coffee and cake or a glass of wine and enjoy the hopefully brilliant sunshine.

Things to see

The statue in Charlotte Square Garden is of Prince Albert, Queen Victoria's consort, and Queen Victoria even came to Edinburgh to do the unveiling in 1876.

Bute House at Number 6 Charlotte Square is the official home of the First Minister of Scotland.

Number 7 is the Georgian House, a National Trust restored house that is open to the public.

Alexander Graham Bell, the man who invented the telephone, lived in South Charlotte Street.

Drinks

Sygn cocktail and dining
15 Charlotte Lane, 0131 225 6060, info@sygn.co.uk
www.sygn.co.uk
Every day 11am to 1am

Sygn is a cocktail bar with warm but minimal interior, stylish patrons and some cocky bar staff who mix–up re-imagined classics. You can buy a bottle of spirits for £50, with mixers and garnish provided – great value for a group. They also do pizzas right up to closing time on Thursdays, Fridays and Saturdays. You could also take part in a 90-minute cocktail masterclass on Thursdays at 7pm and Sundays at 2pm for £25 per person, three cocktails included.

52 Canoes Tiki Bar
13 Melville Place, 0131 226 4732
Monday to Sunday 11am to 1am
If you wondered what a former Irish pub decked out as a Hawaiian hula hut would look like, then here's your answer. Every table is decorated with a kitsch tropical style, there are hibiscus flowers, palms and the glow of pink and yellow lighting. They do Tiki cocktails specialising in rum, good food of the burger-and-nacho variety, and as they describe it, 'sexy banter' with a young, fun crowd.

Bert's Bar
29-31 William Street, 0131 225 5748
www.bertsbar.co.uk
Monday to Wednesday 12pm to 12am, Thursday to Saturday 12am to 1am, Sunday 12.30pm to 12am
One of the popular bars on William Street, Bert's Bar has a great vibe on weekend nights, and if there's a football or rugby game of note on a Saturday afternoon, the pub will be packed with a friendly crowd. It's a traditional looking pub with the hanging baskets outside and they specialise in real ales, with a rotation of nine cask ales on tap.

Teuchters
26 William Street, 0131 225 2973
www.aroomin.co.uk
Monday to Sunday 11am to 1am
On a sunny afternoon, drinkers will spill out the door of Teuchters and onto the pavement of this blue and white corner pub. Teuchter is a nickname for people from the Highlands, and this theme runs through the pub with

an interior decked out like an inn up north, and they sell Scottish beers and whisky. Hearty food is served up in mugs – from chips to haggis and a creamy, coconutty vegetable curry.

Indigo Yard
7 Charlotte Lane, 0131 220 5603
www.indigoyardedinburgh.co.uk
Monday to Saturday 11am to 1am, Sunday to 12.30pm to 1pm
The rumour that they only hire blondes to work in Indigo Yard seems to still hold true – with blonde girls and chiselled robo-boys haughtily working the bar. It's a place that isn't to everyone's taste, with a wealthy, good-looking clientale who have escaped the law firm or architects office. Despite being fashionable it's pretty generic, but the interior stonework inside is interesting and there's a decent patio, which is, confusingly, directly outside the windows of neighbouring Pizza Express.

Restaurants

La P'tite Folie
9 Randolph Place, 0131 225 8678
www.laptitefolie.co.uk
Monday to Saturday 12pm to 3pm and 6pm to 10pm (11pm Friday and Saturday) Closed Sunday
Authentic French restaurant in a uniquely beautiful 19th century mock Tudor house. The ground floor bistro has posters of Amelie and Parisian Art Nouveau, while you climb the stairs to the spacious main restaurant with its simple, stylish décor that blends with the original architectural details of the building, There's also the chance to practice your conversational French with the waiter. Food is classically French, a rack of lamb with nicoise of olives, halibut in a creamy lemongrass and mussel broth, asparagus with parmesan and almonds or tender duck breast with savoy cabbage. Book ahead and ask for the romantic seats in the window alcove.

The Edinburgh Larder

1a Alva Street, 0131 225 4599

Monday to Saturday 12pm to 2.30pm and 5.30pm to 10pm, closed Sunday

With an ethos of using seasonal Scottish ingredients, the Edinburgh Larder is a basement restaurant expanded with a bright, airy conservatory. They do a good value £11.95 set lunch with wholesome rich courses that could include a pate, a fish of the day, foraged herb salads, soft-boiled quails eggs and slow-cooked beef cheek. The food feels very filling but healthy.

Chop Chop

248 Morrison Street, 0131 221 1155

www.chop-chop.co.uk

Monday to Friday 12pm to 2pm and 5.30pm to 10pm, Saturday 12pm to 2pm and 5pm to 10pm, Sunday 12.30pm to 2.30pm and 5pm to 10pm.

A Chinese restaurant in the traditional sense, with speciality dishes from the north eastern provinces. Your table will be laden with food– dumplings, rice, stews, vegetables brought out at different times, depending on when the dishes are ready. So you just dip in and taste whatever arrives first. There's an all you can eat choice, with top-ups of dishes brought to your table and they specialise in jiao zi dumplings – pork and coriander are particularly good. The decoration is also traditional – all red and gold, with Chinese lanterns hanging up.

Cafes and cheap eats

Wannaburger

7 – 8 Queensferry Street, 0131 220 0036

www.wannaburger.com

Everyday 11.30am to 10pm

Avoid the McDonalds and Burger King on Princes Street, and instead nip around the corner for a tastier more authentic burger experience. With bean-burgers, haloumi burgers and chicken burgers on top of the basic burger menu, a range of thick, creamy shakes and with a license to sell beer, Wannaburger is fastfood with a bit more style.

Affogato Gelato e caffe

36 Queensferry Street, 0131 225 1444, admin@affogatogelato.co.uk

www.affogatogelato.co.uk

Tuesday to Thursday 8am to 8pm, Friday 8am to 10pm, Saturday 11am to 10pm, closed Monday

Affogato is vanilla ice-cream in a moat of espresso coffee, and this café specialises in this Italian treat. It's also an Italian gelato experience, with 18 inventive flavours including mojito, gingerbread and chai tea, all created on-site.

Milk

232 Morrison Street, 0131 629 6022, hello@cafemilk.co.uk

www.cafemilk.co.uk

Monday to Friday 7.30am to 4pm, Saturday 8am to 4pm, Sunday 8am to 3pm

Milk aims to provide a wholesome menu in a stripped back interior of wooden benches, plain tiles and coloured seats. There's a chorizo burrito for breakfast, or more nutritious super porridge, eclectic salads, dahls and noodles dishes for lunch and a rotation of homemade cakes on the counter.

Shops

Arkangel and Felon

4 William Street, 0131 226 4466

Monday to Saturday 10am to 5.30pm (6.30pm on Thursday) Closed Sunday

Fashion stylist Sam Cosgrove is co-founder of this independent womenswear boutique that is exclusive Edinburgh stockiest for Almost Famous, Ilse Jacobson and Paul by Paul Smith.

Studio One

10 Stafford Street, 0131 226 5812

www.studio-one.co.uk

Monday to Saturday 10am to 6pm (7pm on Thursday) Sunday 11am to 5pm

Studio One is well-known among Edinburgh locals as the place to come for gifts, especially over Christmas when they stock up on all those cool little stocking fillers such as novelty-shaped chocolates, wicker baskets, wooden toys, jewellery and ceramics. Gift and card shop Paper Tiger, on street level, is owned by the same company.

Artisan Roast

Broughton Street and Cannonmills

Broughton Street is one of Edinburgh's coolest streets, without a chain café or pub in sight. Nestled beneath the old tenements are cafes, restaurants, boutique shops and unique bars and pubs for a cosy pint or to gather pre-club. One of Broughton Streets charms is that while it's only ten minutes walk from Princes Street, it feel almost off the beaten track, and is very much buzzing during the day with workers and residents, and has a great evening atmosphere, whether it's people lingering for the night, or as a pit-stop before moving on elsewhere. It's also gay friendly, forming part of what's known as the pink triangle, extending to CC Blooms nightclub on Leith Walk.

Keep walking down Broughton Street and you will eventually get to Cannonmills, a crossroad which leads to the Botanics, the Water of Leith, King George V Park, Stockbridge and up to Dundas Street.

Drinks

The Phoenix
46 – 48a Broughton Street, 0131 557 0234
Phoenixedinburgh.com
Monday to Saturday 9am to 1am, Sunday 12.30pm to 1am
This Broughton Street stalwart looks like a regular, proper old pub but is a popular, colourful meeting place for weekend drinks and the clubbing crowd. The friendly staff have been there for years, it has a relaxed, sociable feel with a whole spectrum of people, and it's also packed out when rugby and football matches are shown on the big screen.

The Outhouse
12a Broughton Street Lane, 0131 557 6668
www.outhouse-edinburgh.co.uk
Sunday to Thursday 4pm to 1am, Friday and Saturday 12am to 1am

The Outhouse sometimes feels like a secret drinking den in its out-of-the-way location down a cobbled lane just off Broughton Street. With a warm interior glowing by candlelight, it's a pre-club gathering place with a hip young crowd, DJs spinning tunes at the weekends and local artwork for sale. During the summer the weekend Outhouse barbeque in their outdoor patio is a big selling point for those looking for an afternoon hangover recovery of meat, carbs and beer.

The Basement

10a – 12a Broughton Street, 0131 557 0097

www.thebasement.org.uk

Monday to Sunday 12pm to 1am

The Basement is located exactly as its name suggests, hidden below street level. In this popular basement bar with its orange interior and wrought iron chairs, staff in ironic Hawaiian shirts serve up filling food, including huge burritos and enchiladas. There's a steady stream of regulars who often seem to know one another and the servers. In fact all the characters of the place are captured by a large mural on the wall, painted by a former staffer.

Cask and Barrel

115 Broughton Street, 0131 556 3132

Monday to Saturday 11am to 1am, Thursday and Friday 11am to 1am, Sunday 12.30am to 12.30am

The Cask and Barrel is a no-frills real ale house with well priced drinks and with ten traditional ales on taps. A real mix of people come here, from locals propping up the bar to the after-work crowds. If you are lucky you can get a seat outside when sunny and it's a good place to begin a night out, or just to come in and sample some local beers.

Treacle

39-41 Broughton Street, 0131 557 0627

www.treacleedinburgh.co.uk

Everyday 10am to 1am

This hugely popular bar has an eclectic interior with sofas and fluffy cushions, Manga-inspired pop-art on the wall and a raised section to separate the bar floor, for people who want a sit-down meal. The service can be a little slow, but they have a good range of cocktails, an interesting menu, the ubiquitous burgers and bucket of hand-cut chips as well as tempting pan-Asian favourites. There are also a couple of cushioned benches and tables out front for smokers.

Smoke Stack

Restaurants

Smoke Stack
53 Broughton Street, 0131 556 6032
www.smokestack.org.uk
Monday to Thursday 12pm to 2.30pm and 5pm to 10pm, Friday 12am to
11pm, Saturday 11am to 11pm, Sunday 11am to 10pm
If you've got a craving for meat, then the Smoke Stack is the place to come. It's
a self proclaimed "meat-lovers paradise", serving up hearty steaks. Recently
refurbished, the owners have stripped back the interior for exposed stone
walls, wooden floorboards and up-cycled furniture, perhaps with the aim of
creating a lighter interior to compliment the hearty, simple food.

The Olive Branch Bistro
91 Broughton Street, 0131 557 8589
www.theolivebranchscotland.co.uk
Everyday 11.30am to 10pm
With its olive green exterior and bare brick wall interior, the Olive Branch
has a Mediterranean bistro vibe and is very popular for weekend brunches.
The emphasis is on comfort food, with sandwiches, daily pasta dishes, health-
ier cooked breakfasts but also plenty of seafood and meat dishes, such as wild
boar.

Russian Passion
5 Cannonmills, 0131 556 9042
Russianpassioncafe.co.uk
Everyday 11.30am to 3.30pm
This small, unassuming restaurant serves hearty, authentic Russian food
with plenty of buckwheat, rye and sauerkraut, a rare treat to find in Scotland.
Some dishes such as borsch and savoury blini are well-known, others not so
much, such as the chocolate potato, and filled meat piroshky. The owner is
friendly and knowledgeable, it's BYOB and the size of the place means you
should call to book a head. The space can also be booked out for a private
party.

L'escargot Bleu

56 Broughton Street, 0131 557 1600

www.lescargotbleu.co.uk

Monday to Thursday, 12pm to 2.30pm and 5.30pm to 10pm, Friday 12pm to 2.30pm and 5.30pm to 10.30pm, closed Sunday

A French dining room decorated with huge prints of French Art Nouveau posters, serving up food of the Auld Alliance – classic dishes made from local produce. On the menu are duck eggs, prunes soaked in Armagnac, rabbit casserole and rich crème brule. Downstairs is L'Epiceries, a farmhouse style deli crammed with French goodies including cured meats, macarons, French bakery and aperitifs.

Coffee and cheap eats

Artisan Roast

57 Broughton Street, 07526 236 615

www.artisanroast.co.uk

Monday to Thursday 8am to 7.30pm, Friday 8am to 6.30pm, Saturday 9pm to 6.30pm, Sunday 10am to 6.30pm

This tiny little café is a hipster haven of creaking floorboards, cramped tables and a welcoming smell of coffee. Coffee is their business here, and they boast a huge selection of beans from around the world which can be bought wholesale. There are three Artisan Roasts in Edinburgh but Broughton Street is the original, and they even offer live gigs and meditation sessions, which sounds a bit contradictory to the nature of caffeine. Their blackboard on the pavement reflects their quirky outlook on life.

Café Nom de Plum

60 Broughton Street, 0131 478 1372

Monday to Saturday 11am to 10.30pm, Sunday 12pm to 10.30pm

This gay friendly café is above the LGBT centre, and looks inviting with its colourful pot plants and greenery sprouting over the stairs leading up to it, with a menu that takes a trip round the world, and a similarly eclectic interior of faux sunflowers, postal stamp fabric covers, tartan seats, random objects on the mantelpiece and any other available space, and old framed maps.

Casa Angelina
42 London Street, 0131 558 1002
www.casaangelina.co.uk
Tue–Fri 8.45am–6pm, Sat 9am–6pm, Sun 10am–6pm
A vintage-style cake shop with a nicely ironic position in a basement next to the New Town's infamous London Street 'sauna'. It has a cute homebaking feel in the front shop, with cakes such as coconut and mango and lime and mint laid out on a table at the front, with a nicely vintage backroom with garden view, and a cool birdcage print on the wall.

Earthy
1-6 Cannonmills Bridge, 0131 556 9696
www.earthy.uk.com
Monday to Saturday 8am to 8pm, Sunday 9am to 6pm
Earthy is a restaurant serving up locally sourced, seasonal organic food such slow-cooked venison curry and a pear and ginger crumble. There's also a rustic shop attached selling artisan breads, including a seaweed sourdough, fresh fruit and vegetables sourced locally and goods sourced from local producers.

The Circle Café
1 Brandon Terrace, 0131 624 4666, food@thecirclecafe.com
Monday to Thursday 8.30am to 4.30pm, Friday and Saturday 8.30am to 10pm, Sunday 9am to 4.30pm
The Circle, with its stonewall interior and back window overlooking their garden, is a great place to come for breakfast, opposite the big clock at Cannonmills. At the weekends, tables are snapped up quickly, but it's worth checking out, whether for reading the paper over one of their semi-circle and full circle breakfasts, or to come in for a take-away coffee and a giant croissant or pain au chocolat.

Urban Angel
1 Forth Street, 0131 556 6323, info@urban-angel.co.uk
Monday to Saturday 9am to late, Sunday 9am to 5pm
121 Hanover Street, 0131 556 6323, info@urban-angel.co.uk
Monday to Saturday 9am to 5pm, Sunday 10am to 5pm

www.urban-angel.co.uk

With two locations in the New Town, café/bistro Urban Angel is good for coffee and cake or a healthy brunch, it's seasonal and organic, and the specials chance regularly. The interior is clean, white and minimal, and with tempting salads and cakes and tarts, such as plum frangipani tart, on display by the counter, it's the food that makes the impact.

Coffee Angel

24 – 27 Brandon Terrace, 0131 622 6235, info@coffee-angel.co.uk

www.coffee-angel.co.uk

Monday to Friday 7.30am to 7pm, Saturday 8.30am to 7pm, Sunday 10am to 7pm

Run by a brother and sister team, Coffee Angel is a popular Cannonmills café for mothers with their buggies, families, and workers from some of the businesses nearby, and while the food is fairly standard with sandwiches and paninis, they have great tasting lattes and an imaginative range of drinks including iced coffee, orange mocha and honey and vanilla chai latte.

Joey D

Jars of marshmallow crafted by The Marshmallow Lady, photo Nicola Roberts

Shops

Crombies of Edinburgh
97-101 Broughton Street, 0131 556 7643, mail@sausages.co.uk
www.sausages.co.uk
Monday to Friday 8am to 5.30pm, Saturday 8am to 5pm, Sunday closed
Well-loved Crombies is a local butcher with a huge variety (over 40) of home-made sausages. The One O Clock Banger, in tribute to Edinburgh's One O Clock gun, definitely has a kick to it, and it's a great to stop by and pick up half a kilo if you are on your way to a barbeque. You can also buy haggis from here, the recipe for which dates back to 1920.

Real Foods
37 Broughton Street, 0131 557 1911, admin@realfoods.co.uk
www.realfoods.co.uk
Monday to Friday 8am to 9pm, Saturday 9am to 6.30pm, Sunday 10am to 6pm

This health food store, originally opened in the 1970s, is a treasure trove for health aficionados. There are large sacks of different types of muesli, a huge selection of every conceivable dried fruit, nut and seed, plus organic produce and hard to find products.

Coco Chocolate
71 Broughton Street, 0131 558 2777, info@cocochocolate.co.uk
www.cocochocolate.co.uk
Monday to Saturday 10am to 6pm, Sunday 12pm to 5pm
A little shop selling hand-crafted high-cocoa chocolate in pretty packaging, all made in Edinburgh. You can also try your hand at making your own at their chocolate school. There are also tasting evenings to learn all about chocolate, sample cocoa nibs, cocoa butter and Madagascan beans, served with a glass of 1994 Mas Amiel. If you are really obsessed by chocolate, there are one day chocolate courses at the Coco Chocolate school in Roslin, just outside Edinburgh.

The Marshmallow Lady
14 Rodney Street, 07843 699 790
www.burghbakes.com
Wednesday to Friday 12pm to 6pm, Saturday 11 to 6pm
Edinburgh's first Marshmallow shop sells a fun confection of homemade squares of gourmet mallows, from Millionaire Shortbread and lemon meringue, to the more obscure Innis and Gunn beer variety. They are all made in the kitchen at the back of the shop by owner Nicole Roberts, and there is a café serving marshmallow milkshakes and lemonade. They are great for gifts or just as a sweet treat a world away from the pink and white bags you can buy in the supermarket.

The Dragonfly Gifts
111a Broughton Street, 0131 629 4246, dragonflyarts@btinternet.com
www.thedragomnflygifts.co.uk
Monday to Wednesday, Friday and Saturday 11am to 6pm, Thursday 10am to 7pm, Sunday 1pm to 7pm

CAROLINE YOUNG

This retro and vintage style boutique has a good mix of gifts as well as a boutique selling funky dresses, cardigans and blouses from brands such as Yummi, jewellery from local artists, children's clothing by Belle and Boo, printed bags and purses and quirky cards and novelty objects.

Indie and Chic
111 Broughton Street, 0131 558 1757, hello@indiechicboutique.co.uk
www.indiechicboutique.co.uk
Monday 12pm to 5pm, Tuesday to Saturday 11am to 6pm (Thursday until 7.30pm), Sunday 12pm to 5pm
This boutique sells lux silk and lace lingerie, dresses and tops by cult brands imported from Los Angeles, Miami and San Francisco. The clothes have a classic, vintage 1930s and 40s feel to them and they specialise in beautiful soft bras without padding or underwire.

Joey D
54 Broughton Street, 0131 557 6672, joey@joey-d.co.uk
www.joey-d.co.uk
Monday to Sunday 10.30am to 6pm
Unique fashion designer Joey D sells one-off punky deconstructed clothing recycled from vintage materials. There are paint-splashed shirts, ripped denim, different fabrics stitched together, leather satchels and bags made from Doc Marten boots. His kilts even take part in the Dressed to Kilt show every year in New York.

Concrete Wardrobe
50a Broughton Street, 0131 558 7130, concretewardrobe@hotmail.co.uk
www.concretewardrobe.com
Monday to Saturday 11am to 7pm, Sunday 12pm to 5pm
This Scottish-designed crafts store was opened in 2000 by textile designer Fiona McIntosh and weaver James Donald. Designs are inspired by the wilds of Scotland, including stag broaches, heron prints, Scottish fabrics in scarves and drapes, and hand-made Scottish ceramics.

White Rabbit

44 Broughton Street, 0131 557 6819 shop@white-rabbit-edinburgh.com

white-rabbit-edinburgh.com

Monday 12pm to 4.30pm, Tuesday to Thursday 12pm to 6.30pm, Friday to Sunday 12pm to 7pm

One of the most recent additions to Broughton Street, White Rabbit brings some much needed erotica to the area, but it's not typical Ann Summers – it does it with intelligent artistic style and a vintage, burlesque feel. There are leather and lace underwear, artwork, Victorian erotic literature and of course sex toys and strange contraptions, all in this "den of decadence."

Curious and Curiouser

93 Broughton Street, 0131 556 1866, shop@curiouserandcuriouser.com

Tuesday to Saturday 10am to 6pm, Sunday and Monday 12pm to 4pm

With a name evoking Alice in Wonderland, Curious and Curiouser is a gift and art shop, with one of the best selections of imaginative cards. A woodland theme of deer, owls, foxes runs through many of the homeware gifts and jewellery, felt placemats and coasters, and there also picture frames and prints, with some Edinburgh themes.

Elaine's Vintage Clothing on St Stephen's Street

STOCKBRIDGE

Stockbridge, recently named by The Times as one of Britain's coolest places to live, is a ramshackled village for artists and creative types with its cobbled streets, Georgian terraces, colony housing, delis and vintage shops, and the Water of Leith cutting right through. It's a place that is popular with students and young singles, but also has one of the most expensive streets in Edinburgh with Ann Street, where a townhouse on this Raeburn designed street can set you back £1.5 million. As well as being a desirable place to live, it's also a fun place to go out for drinks, with a number of great bars within hopping distance.

Despite one national supermarket, a heavy dose of charity shops and several coffee chains, Stockbridge has managed to retain a sense of independence, partly down to pro-active residents being up in arms with any conglomerate coming into the area. Michelin star chef Tom Kitchin's new gastro-pub has notched up the cool factor, the weekend market appeals to foodies and those who are into the street food revolution, and has the alluringly seedy history of being best known for the Danube Street brothel, run by Madame Dora Noyce.

Stockbridge has a real bohemian vibe, a 70s hippy feel to it, and the people who have made it their home at one time include Garbage frontwoman Shirley Manson (who went to nearby Broughton High), musician Finley Quay, novelist Ann Fine, Rab C Nesbitt actor Gregor Fisher and even Nico, the Warhol superstar and singer for Velvet Underground. Comedian Dylan Moran from sitcom Black Books can also be spotted around the area.

Another famous name is Madame Doubtfire, who ran a rag and bone shop in the 1920s on South East Circus Place, which is now the Doubtfire

Gallery. Anne Fine was inspired to write her novel, later loosely adapted into the Robin Williams film, from her time living in a draughty Dundas Street flat in the 1970s. She would pass by the old shop with its musty interior, and the proprietor was often seen sitting outside her shop, smoking a pipe and wrapped in shawls.

Things to see

The Stockbridge Duck Race, a tradition since the 1980s, takes place every June on the Water of Leith. Anyone can participate by buying a rubber duck from one of the shops with a number on it, and prizes are donated by local businesses.

The Stockbridge Market takes place every Sunday in the space by Saunders Street. This market is a bustling place to snack on hot foods, buy fresh lemonade, cakes, artisan bread and jewellery from the stalls nestled under trees. Sometimes there is live music, and there is always a delicious smell in the air of meats and curry being cooked.

Cobbled, winding Ann Street, one of the oldest streets in the area, was named after painter Henry Raeburn's wife. Raeburn bought two estates, Deanhaugh and St Bernard's, in the 1790s, and with architect James Milne, they designed the foundations of Stockbridge.

St Stephen Street was once a run-down area known for its antique shops. The basement shops are believed to originally have been brothels, or dens of ill-repute. It has that mix of rough and refined that makes St Stephen's Street the place to come for a taste of bohemia and some quirky shopping.

Just off St Stephen's Street is the entrance to the old Stockbridge Market.

Dora Noyce was madame of a brothel at 17 Danube Street which had a roaring trade from the 2nd World War through to the 1970s. Its busiest times were reportedly during the festival and the annual gathering of the Church of Scotland.

St Stephen's Church at the bottom of Howe Street, its imposing bell tower jutting upwards, marks the entrance to Stockbridge. It was designed by William Playfair in 1827.

Pretty Gloucester Lane was the birthplace of artist David Roberts, and it's worth a ramble with its cobbles and mismatched mews houses.

The Danish Cultural Institute at 3 Doune Terrace holds events and Danish themed exhibitions and film screenings. www.dancult.co.uk

There's a very nice stretch along the Water of Leith to Dean Village, passing 17th century Lindsay's Mill, one of 11 water powered mills for grain. The route goes under the imposing Dean Bridge with its huge arches. You then enter into Dean Village from Miller Row, which has the feel of a Swiss village.

Also along this stretch of the Water of Leith is St Bernard's Well, designed by painter Alexander Naysmith in 1789, after a natural spring with health giving properties was discovered. Based on the Temple of Vesta in Trivoli, it has a statue of Hygeia, the Greek goddess of health, and where the word 'hygiene' comes from.

The Stockbridge Colonies were built between 1861 and 1911 as artisan housing built by the Edinburgh Co-Operative Building Company. The colonies have become a pretty trendy, desirable place to live despite the threat of flooding from the nearby Water of Leith.

The Old Stockbrisge Market entrance, photo C Young

The Scran and Scallie

Restaurants

The Stockbridge Restaurant
54 St Stephen Street, 0131 226 6766
Tuesday to Thursday 7pm to 9.30pm, Friday and Saturday 6.30pm to 9.30pm, Sunday 7pm to 9pm. Closed Monday.
The Stockbridge Restaurant has the feel of an Edinburgh New Town living room, with dark walls, plush drapes and paintings on the wall. The Ivy covered and fairy lit steps down to the entrance also adds to the romanticism. The menu by owner and chef Jason Gallagher offers rich, meaty, artfully presented and textured dishes – a grilled halibut with crab risotto, avocado ice-cream and langoustine sauce, rabbit loin wrapped in Serrano ham, pork fillets wrapped in pancetta, with pork belly, cheeks and black pudding. The palette cleansers between courses are also a nice touch, as well as bread served with a chive, chervil and olive oil dip.

The Scran and Scallie
1 Comely Bank Road, 0131 332 6281
Monday to Sunday 10am to 10pm
The Scran and Scallie is new gourmet pub from the people behind The Kitchin and Castle Terrace Restaurant. They've gone for a pub favourites menu, and while haddock, chips and tartare sauce will set you back £14, it's superior pub food with oysters, pig ear pork scratchings, and blood orange jelly and ice-cream for desert. They have broad Scots labellings on the menu to add to the earthiness, although the prices take pub food up a notch.

Bell's Diner
7 St Stephen Street, 0131 225 8116
Open 6pm to 10.30pm Mon-Fri, Sun; noon-10.30pm Sat.
Bell's Diner has been serving up burgers and steaks since 1972. The burger portions are huge, with their famed butter toppings to add to succulence, and you can have the burgers in a variety of different ways. Steaks are supplied by Allan Campbell's butchery in nearby Boswall Parkway.

Cafes and snacks

The Pantry
1-2 North West Circus Place, 0131 629 0206
Monday to Sunday 8.30am to 9.30pm
An urban farm shop and kitchen using Scottish sourced ingredients. The interior is going for a kitchen vibe with its wooden tables and tiled floor. A different 'stewp' – which is a cross between a stew and soup – is served up daily.

Peter's Yard
3 Deanhaugh Street, 0131 332 2901
www.petersyard.com
Monday to Friday 8am to 9pm, Saturday and Sunday 9am to 9pm
This Swedish bakery says it is inspired by the idea of Fika, a Swedish word for meeting for food, coffee and chat. They specialise in sourdough pizza, baked in their pizza oven, and their award-winning sourdough crispbread is also, stocked in hotels and restaurants in the UK. With a busy atmosphere, wide tables that can be shared with strangers and a bustling counter stocked with freshly made pastries, cakes, sandwiches, and sourdough and granary loafs to take-away.

Drinks

The Antiquary
72 – 78 St Stephen Street, 0131 225 2858
www.theantiquarybar.co.uk
Monday 11.30am to 11pm, Tuesday to Wednesday 11.30am to 12.30am, Sunday 12.30pm to 12.30pm
A traditional pub with a name that comes from the poem by Sir Walter Scott (his painting hangs on the wall), the Antiquary has that old-school pub feel and smell. The cellar holds the remains of a 19th century bakery and it's been rumoured that the pub is haunted by the friendly spirits of a lady baker and her son. The left side entrance to the bar has a different look to the newer right hand side – more of a dark, antique feel. It's been a place for the

hippies of the Stockbridge, the biker community of the 80s, the hard drinking Happy Humpers technicians of the live music scene and The Animals of the 1990s.

The Bailie

2 – 4 St Stephen Street, 0131 225 4673

A traditional community pub where students and old regulars converge for a quiet pint, to take part in the pub quiz on Tuesdays or to hear live music on Friday nights. The Bailie is believed to have been a pub since the 1870s, bought by poet Hamish Henderson and named The Bailie in 1971 after a theatre production. They serve Scottish cask ales from local breweries, and typical pub food has been smartened up - haddock is IPA battered, the fishcakes have chorizo.

Last Word cocktail saloon

44 St Stephen Street, 0131 225 9009

Monday to Sunday 4pm to 1am

www.lastwordsaloon.com

7 days, 4pm – 1am

From the same guys who own Bramble, The Last Word pays tribute to the 1920s prohibition era speakeasy, and as it gets dark outside, the lights dim and the bar, with its old world feel, is lit by the glow of candlelight. The cocktails aren't they type that come with an umbrella, they are the real deal – served simple and strong, interestingly mixed and unique liquors, such as black bottle whisky with cream soda, and their signature Last Word cocktail, originally created at the Detroit Athletic Club – fifty pounds, green chartreuse, maraschino liqueur and fresh lime juice.

Hector's in Stockbridge

47-49 Deanhaugh Street, 0131 343 1735

Monday to Wednesday 12pm to 12am, Thursday and Friday, 12pm to 1am, Saturday 11am to 1am, Sunday 11am to 12am

Hector's holds court as one of the most popular bar in Stockbridge – which in turn is one of the trendiest, desirable places to stay in Edinburgh. It has the atmosphere of a hip, friendly local – a place to drop in for a cocktail, to try out of their six real ales they have on tap, to gorge on a Sunday roast, and to relax for brunch at the weekends.

Hamilton's Bar and Kitchen
16 to 18 Hamilton Place, 0131 226 4199
9am to 1am, 7 days a week
One of the most popular bars in Stockbridge for young trendies, Hamilton's has huge leather sofas to sink into, and huge Pop Art murals on the walls and in the menus, a treat for Roy Lichenstein fans, with their images of coy blondes and tough, be-suited men. Hamilton's serve up good bar food with a tasty sweet potato and bean burger with parsnip fries, although booking a table is advised if you want to eat there, as they get snapped up quickly. Cocktail themes pay tribute to Rebel Without a Cause, Blue Hawaii, sugary Pillow Talk and the darker and dirtier Guns, Girls and Gangsters.

Photo courtesy of Hamilton's Bar and Restaurant

Those Were The Days vintage boutique

Shops

Vox Box
21 St Stephen Street, 0131 6296775
Wednesday to Friday 12 to 5pm, Saturday 10.30am to 5pm, Sunday 12pm
to 4pm
www.voxboxmusic.co.uk
Opened in 2011, Vox Box is a clean, uncluttered, white-walled record store
which celebrates vinyl with almost mint second-hand records and some brand
new, in genres including punk, blue, jazz and folk. They don't sell techno and
dance music though. The backroom has boxes of bargain Vinyl, including
7-inch singles, to rummage through.

Sheila Fleet Gallery
18 St Stephen Street, 0131 225 5939
www.sheilafleet.com
Monday to Saturday 10am to 5.30pm, closed Sunday
Orkney jewellery designer Sheila Fleet designs and makes her jewellery
in rural Orkney, as inspired by the sea, the barren landscape, wild grasses
and the Viking history of the island. It's a family run business and one
of the biggest employers on the island. The gallery holds the largest collection outside of Orkney and also showcases ceramics by other Scottish
designers.

Those were the days Vintage
26 St Stephen Street, 0131 225 4400
Monday to Saturday 11am to 6pm, Sunday 12pm to 5pm
Styling itself as a vintage lover's paradise, this boutique sells funky vintage
wear from the 1930s to the 80s, all sourced from around the world. You can
find glitzy 70s Studio 54 styling, 1950s prom dresses, sharp 60s coats and
heaps of beautiful accessories. The racks are not over-crammed so it's easy
to search out the treasures. They also stock art deco jewellery, Bakelite and
Lucite as well as 80s and 90s Chanel, Givenchy and Dior.

Hibiscus flower

48 St Stephen Street, 0131 225 4211

www.hibiscusflower.co.uk

Closed Monday

Tuesday to Friday 10.30am to 5.30pm, Saturday 10am to 5.30pm, Sunday 12pm to 5pm

Specialising in ethical women's clothing, Hibiscus Flower only sells garments and accessories that comply with international Fairtrade standards, and stocks brands such as People Tree, Komodo and Peter Jensen.

Elaine's vintage clothing

55 St Stephen Street, 0131 225 5783

Closed Monday

Crossing through the mint green Art Nouveau shutters, is like entering into another-worldy place – Mr Ben brought to life. This vintage store is eccentric, bohemian, eclectic and great fun searching through the goods that conjure up visions of old Hollywood glamour.

Cherubim

68 St Stephen Street, 0131 225 8242

www.edinburgh-cherubim.co.uk

Wednesday to Saturday 11am to 6pm, Sunday 11am to 5pm, closed Monday and Tuesday

Very cool and unique vintage furniture pieces on display in this shop specialising in brocante furniture and contemporary Scottish art. A yellow 70s drink cabinet, a 1930s bureau, a sky blue coffee table featuring a world were just some of the items hand selected for display by the owners who have experience as artists and furniture makers.

IJ Mellis

6 Bakers Place, 0131 225 6566, info@ijmellischeesemonger.com

Mellischeese.co.uk

Monday to Friday 9am to 6.30pm, Saturday 9am to 6pm, Sunday 12pm to 5pm

There are several branches of this cheesemonger around Edinburgh. It has a reputation as the place to go for cheese and you can certainly smell its pungency as you approach. With huge rolls of cheese stacked up, you can explore Scottish cheeses including Mull cheddar.

Chic and Unique
8 Deanhaugh Street, 0131 332 9889
Tuesday to Saturday 10.30am to 5pm
www.vintagecostumejewellery.co.uk/shop/
Chic and Unique is a treasure-trove of vintage costume jewellery, scarves and Venetian carnival masks. There are beautiful Art Deco dress clips and bracelets, necklaces from the 1930s, Art Nouveau pieces, hat pins, designs from the 1950s by Trifari and 1980s broaches. While many are collector's pieces, you can also find items for under £30.

Sculleries of Stockbridge
25 North West Circus Place, 0131 226 6670
Monday 12pm to 4.30pm, Tuesday to Saturday 10am to 5pm, closed Sunday
This kitchen design shop also sells handmade wooden objects including ghost-like spatulas, pig shaped and Scotty-dog chopping boards if you are looking for a little gift for someone back home.

Daisy Cheynes
51 Raeburn Place, 0131 629 6758, Karen.heriot@daisycheynes.com
www.daisycheynes.com
Monday to Saturday 9.30am to 5.30pm, Sunday 12pm to 5pm
A selection of products from around Scotland including soaps from North Uist, slate chalkboards from Fife and cards featuring Scottish icons like the Highland Cow and Irn Bru can.

LEITH

Leith is Edinburgh's port, a dockland with a rowdy, rough reputation and history as the main access point by sea for Scotland, and a major base for whaling and manufacturing.

Leith and the Shore is also synonymous with the works of writer Irvine Welsh, the place where his junkie characters live and play, and certainly in the 1980s it had a reputation for its big drug problem.

From 1833 to 1920 it was an independent burgh and it still has that sense of being separate from the rest of the city. Leith is also unofficially is twinned with Rio de Janeiro. This makes sense as Leith is the wilder, party place in the city and there are several festivals that take place down that way several times a year.

Leith has a real multi-cultural vibe, with an influx of Polish people in the last decade, and a Punjabi community merging with the strong working class Scottish ethic.

For centuries the area was a cramped, thriving port with slums and packed tenements, but with the decline of industry and as the slums have been cleared, Leith has seen a revival and gentrification. You are more likely to find design and ad agencies, and lawyers' offices down in Leith, and with that comes the young and affluent buying up flats.

Like the Meat-packing district in New York, what was once a seedy area with warehouses, the Shore has been done-up and now has some of the best restaurants in the country and a concentration of Michelin stars.

The Shore, with its cobbled streets, gabled buildings and bars with tables spilling out onto the pavement, has the quaint atmosphere of a sailor's port gone up market, but still with that rough underbelly.

Down by shopping centre Ocean Terminal is a derelict wasteland of half-empty apartments, with the plan for swanky sea view homes scuppered by the recession. Maybe once the economy picks up, this barren wind-swept area will be developed once again.

The soundtrack to Leith has to be the Proclaimer's The Sunshine on Leith, from 1988. The title track was a love song to this area of Edinburgh, the place where they grew up, and it is still played by local football team Hibs at the beginning of matches. Their album Sunshine on Leith features the hit that's brought in the royalties for them, I'm Gonna Be (500 Miles), which was not really heard outside of Scotland until it was included on the soundtrack to quirky Johnny Depp movie Benny and Joon in 1993.

Leith was at one time the base for the largest whaling fleet in the world, Christian Salvesan and Co, which began operating in 1908. Whaling was one of the big employers in the area and the oil was important for manufacturing for use in oil lamps and in soap. Leith was also the home of Rose's Lime Juice, founded in 1860 and provided to all ships required by law to have lime on board.

Leith has seen some famous characters from history pass through. In 1561 Mary Queen of Scots arrived in Leith after arriving back from France, but because she was early, no one was there to meet her, so she stayed at the house of Andrew Lamb. King James VI and his new Queen, Anne of Denmark, arrived in 1590 after being married in Oslo. Oliver Cromwell also set up residence at the Citadel after the Battle of Dunbar in 1649. George IV landed at the Shore in 1822 to huge welcome, including being greeted Sir Walter Scott. And of course in 1998, Leith became the permanent of the Royal Yacht Britannia, launched in 1953 and the Windsor family residence on sea for over 40 years.

The founder of the US Navy John Paul Jones almost made it to Leith – during the War of Independence, he sailed up the Forth with the aim of taking control of the port, but their plan was stopped by a storm.

The rules of golf are also said to originate in Leith – they were written up in 1744 for a tournament on Leith Links.

Things to see

Leith's history of seafaring, whaling and as a vital port of arrival for trade and VIPs is still evident.

The Sailor's Home, now the Malmaison Hotel, was opened in 1833 as a place of recovery for seaman, officers and even those who needed to recover from being shipwrecked.

There's a harpoon down on the Shore which is a symbol and reminder for Leith's whaling history.

Lamb's House, recently sold by the National Trust for Scotland to an expert restorer after years of neglect, is thought to date back to the mid 16th century, partly because of the account of Mary Queen of Scots staying at Lamb's House, although the architecture is 17th century. It was once the finest home in Leith, originally owned by merchant Andrew Lamb, featuring gables, tall chimneys and large fireplaces, and with a warehouse attached.

Rose's lime juice was originally manufactured on Commercial Street from 1860, to provide to the ships that were required by law to have lime onboard, as a way to prevent scurvy. (This is where the American nickname for Brits, Limeys, comes from.) Limes were processed in the Dominican Republic, and it was so popular that it branched out to the Gold Coast. It was bought by Schweppes in 1955, which was bought by Cadbury's, who have in turn been bought over by Kraft.

The Citadel at 175 Commercial Street, now a youth centre, was built for Oliver Cromwell in the 1650s when he ruled Scotland from London. At the foot of the walk was originally Central Station.

The King's Wark is the oldest building in the Shore, founded by James I in 1434 as a storeroom, and originally a tower on the site of where the restaurant is now. The tower was destroyed by fire around 1690 and the current building went up soon after.

The Signal Tower, on top of Fishers restaurant, was built as a windmill around 1685. Its dome and sails were taken away in 1805, and it let ships know the level of the water as they came into the harbour.

The Rose Leaf

THE SHORE

Drinks

The Rose Leaf
23/24 Sandport Place, 0131 476 5268
www.roseleaf.co.uk
Sunday to Thursday 10am to 12am, Friday and Saturday 10am to 1am
One of the friendliest pubs down the Shore, The Rose Leaf has a kitch, antique
vibe with a highlight being the pot-tails – refreshing cocktails served in a
teapot, with a teacup and saucer. The front half of the bar is for lively, sociable drinks while the section at the back is for a quieter sit-down meal. They
can also organise fun Mad Hatter's tea parties, with cocktails instead of the
tea and a random mix of hats (normally hung up on the wall) for guests to
wear.

Bond No.9
84 Commercial Street, 0131 555 5578, info@bondno9.co.uk
www.bondno9.co.uk
Everyday 12pm to 1am
Bond No.9 gets its name from being on the site of old whisky bonds, rather
than from 007. Although slightly pretentious, it adds some sophistication to
raucous Leith while still embracing the fun of the area, with some decadent
champagne and absinthe cocktails that would make a sailor lose his sea legs.
They've kept the original wood beam features but given it a sophisticated,
lounge style.

Sofi's Bar

65 Henderson Street 0131 555 7019, sofis@bodabar.com

www.bodabar.com

Monday to Friday 2pm to 1am, Saturday 12pm to 1am, Sunday 1pm to 1am

With its duck egg blue and lemon yellow walls, floral curtains, faded stylish-ness – Sofi's bar seems like a little shabby chic ray of sunshine. This intimate little bar is part of the group of Swedish bars, fast becoming a Leith institu-tion. They organise knitting nights, show free film with popcorn in the small room at the back and there's a vinyl party where you can bring along records and have a go on the decks.

Teuchters Landing

1c Dock Place, 0131 554 7427

www.aroomin.co.uk

Everyday 10.30am to 1am

This bar has a funky location in a converted wooden boathouse, and they have a mug menu which serves up chips, haggis, curries, macaroni cheese and ice-cream in mugs. It has a lively atmosphere, and several smaller rooms with seats off the main bar, an outdoor area at the front and a floating pontoon for terrace drinks.

Nobles

44a Constitution Street, 0131 629 7215

www.noblesbarleith.co.uk

Monday to Saturday 11am to 1m, Sunday 10am to 1am.

Nobles, with its open floor space, stained-glass windows, and mahogany keeps the ship theme with images of sails in the stained glass, ship models up around the bar, and an eclectic, stylish interior. As well as being a lively bar with regular live music in the evenings, it is also well known for excellent breakfasts and brunches.

Port O Leith

58 Constitution Street, 0131 554 3568

Monday to Thursday 11am to 1am, Friday and Saturday 9am to 1am, Sunday 12.30pm to 1am

With a ceiling covered in flags, walls decorated with life jackets, raucous dancing on the bar on weekend nights, Port o Leith is one of the most characterful pubs on the Shore. A mix of the rough, tough and the trendy all converge together for a fun and often eventful evening. Irvine Welsh has been known to pop in from time to time. The red exterior was painted green when it was being used as a location for film Sunshine on Leith, causing outrage amongst Heart fans, as their colour is maroon, while rival Hibs is green.

The Shore Bar
3 Shore, 0131 553 5080
www.fishersbistros.co.uk
12pm until late
The Shore has a port bar feel with its dark wood interior, a swing door entrance a polished wood interior, and a deceptive mirror at the back of the bar, as if on an old-fashioned cruise ship. They serve ales, good seafood and live music and there is a separate, more formal, dining room.

Restaurants

The Ship on the Shore
24-26 The Shore, 0131 555 0409, seafood@theshipontheshore.co.uk
www.theshipontheshore.co.uk
Every day 12pm to 10pm, and a Ship's breakfast everyday 9am to 11am
With a plush interior of plum velvet and dark wood, white table clothes and vases of flowers, this champagne bar and seafood restaurant has the feel of a ship's dining room from years gone by. Their ethos is for customers to drink champagne with the finest seafood in a relaxed setting, and they have a special crustacean and mollusks menu to be enjoyed with their house champagne Ruinart Brut. A dinner menu serves Scottish classics like Cullen Skink, Aberdeen smoked haddock, and Scottish smoked salmon. They have changing works of art up on the wall, and the tables outside are made from the varnished wood from wine crates.

Mithas
7 Dock Place, 0131 554 0008, dine@mithas.co.uk
Mithas.co.uk

Tuesday Sunday, lunch 12pm to 2.30pm, dinner 5.30pm to 10pm

Mithas offers a glamorous taste of India from the people behind the famous Khushi's. The Mhugal style interior and special tasting menu is a cut above the average Indian restaurant, with Monkfish or Spinach and Fig Tikki, Tawa Lobster and Venison kebab. They do BYOB with no corkage, but prefer people to only bring wine.

Monday to Thursday 12pm to 11pm, Friday and Saturday 12pm to 12am, Sunday 11am to 11pm.

36 Shore, 0131 554 9260

In one of the oldest buildings in Leith, its origins dating back to the 15th century, The King's Wark has a great reputation for good, hearty food, a cosy old-inn style atmosphere of oak tables and candlelight. You can book a table in the restaurant at the back, but finding a table for food by the bar is done on a first come first served basis, and it does get very busy. But you can always have a drink by the bar while you wait. The Haggis and Fish and Chips are solid favourite.

Coffee and cheap eats

Mimi's Bake House

63 Shore, 0131 555 5908, info@mimisbakehouse.com

www.mimisbakehouse.com

Monday – Friday 9am to 5pm, Saturday and Sunday 9am to 6pm

Mimi's is a mouthwatering, retro girly slice of cake, with a devoted local following. The décor is giant humbug meets pink parlour, with black and white stripes, and cerise and black sofas. The counter displays luscious, giant slabs of cake – oaty fudge bars, malteser cake. They also do a filling selection of savoury food including an incredibly thick quiche-style savoury tart. To keep up with the 50s feel, they sell mugs and bags by Dupenny, who also designed the cheeky pin-up wallpaper.

Shops

Flux

55 Bernard Street, 0131 554 4075, bea@get2flux.co.uk

www.get2flux.co.uk

Monday to Saturday 11am to 6pm, Sunday 12pm to 5pm

With its chintzy wallpaper entrance way, Flux is a treat of a gift shop, selling quirky gifts that come with an all-ethical guarantee. Products include a Wall's Ice Cream satchel, pink flamingo lights and a necklace with Scots words like blether and numpty.

The Ship on the Shore

The King's Wark

Joseph Pearce

Leith Walk

Leith Walk is the multi-cultural hub of Edinburgh, with Chinese supermarkets, Polish delis, Swedish pubs, and Indian textile shops ad amongst the grocery shops and old man pubs. The Foot of the Walk has a rough reputation, but it becomes more gentrified and the bars more stylised, the further up you go.

Drinks

Boda Bar
229 Leith Walk, 0131 553 5900, boda@bodabar.com
www.bodabar.com
Monday to Friday 2pm – 1am, Saturday 12pm – 1am, Sunday 1pm to 12am. One of the Swedish chain of bars, Boda has cushioned seat by the window, fairy lighting around the bar, and a lively, friendly atmosphere. They serve up Green and Black's hot cocoa, Swedish cider and huge variety of beers and cocktails. There is live music on Monday's and they organise regular event including bar boot sales.

Victoria
265 Leith Walk, 0131 555 1638, boda@bodabar.com
www.bodabar.com
Monday to Friday 2pm to 1am, Saturday 1pm to 1am, Sunday 1pm to 12am
Another of the Swedish chain of stylish pubs, Victoria's is laidback and cool, and with regular events including singles nights, Come Dine with me themed even and Eurovision celebrations. It has the eclectic interior of comfy sofas, fairy lights, cushioned window benches and local artwork and fashion displayed up on the walls.

Robbies Bar
367 Leith Walk, 0131 554 6850
Monday to Friday 12pm to 12am, Saturday 11am to 12am, Sunday 12.30am to 12am
Not wanting to pay upscale drink prices? Robbie's is good value, a basic pub with old Leith Walk characters, Hibs fans and a wall covered in old

photographs. This is how pubs on Leith Walk were before the gentrification, and worth a visit to get a different perspective from visiting the Swedish pubs.

Joseph Pearce

23 Elm Row, 0131 556 4140, jp@bodabar.com

www.bodabar.com

Sunday to Thursday 11am to 12am, Friday and Saturday 11am to 1am

Joseph Pearce's is one of the set of Swedish bars that has defined the gentrification of Leith Walk. Taking over the old-man stalwart at the top of the walk, it has become a hugely popular local meeting hub and a landmark in the area in its own right for the cool crowd. They serve a Swedish and Scottish menu, assorted types of seats, organised events including jogging and scrabble. The seating outside on a summer's day gets snapped up fast, but they are thoughtful enough to hand out blankets when the Edinburgh summer chill kicks in. It has a slightly magical air to it, with menus in fairytale books, floral wallpaper and decorative birdcages.

The Tourmalet

25 Buchanan Street, 0131 555 4387

Monday and Tuesday 3pm to 12am, Wednesday to Friday 3pm to 1am, Saturday and Sunday 1pm to 1am

The Tourmalet is a bar that pays tribute to cycling, with its name coming from a section of the Tour de France, as well as specialising in German wheat beer. Cycling and other less popular sports are played on the telly, and it's a popular bar with a young local crowd and some older characters, giving it a good weekend vibe.

Elbow

East Claremont Street, 0131 556 5662, elbowedinburgh@googlemail.com

www.elbowedinburgh.co.uk

Monday to Sunday 11am to 1am

Just a five minutes stroll from Leith Walk, Elbow is an eclectic lively pub, with an unexpectedly funky loft style interior, if you judged it from its nondescript façade on a quiet street. It becomes a real party place at the weekend, with local DJs doing pre-club warm-ups. Saturday night Soul Kitchen plays funk, soul and hip-hop from 9pm. The crowd is cool, knowledgeable of the club scene and up for a good time.

Restaurants

La Favorita
325-331 Leith Walk, 0131 554 2430, santeb@vittoriarestaurant.com
www.vittoriagroup.co.uk
Everyday 12pm to 11pm
One of the most popular restaurants down Leith Walk, this pizzeria does crisp wood-fired pizzas (some consider the best in town) in a minimalist setting where you can see the dough being worked on by the chefs at the front of house.

Pomegranate
1 Antigua Street, 0131 556 8337, pomegranate-edinburgh@hotmail.com
Pomegranatesrestaurant.com
Monday to Sunday 12am to 12pm
With its garish pink and green interior, Pomegranate stands out with its jeweled colours at the top of Leith Walk. They specialise in Middle Eastern street food from countries including Saudi Arabia, Lebanon, Iraq, Iran and Morocco, where you can choose a four, five or six dish mezze platter, trying such treats as baba ghanoush, tapenade, mince lamb with rice and sultana, falafel or spy Lebanese sausage. For after dinner they have Arabic coffee or a puff on their shisha pipes on their dedicated shisha terrace outside.

Khushi's Indian Restaurant
10 Antigua Street, 0131 558 1947, dine@khushis.com
www.khushis.com
Sunday to Thursday 12pm to 10pm, Friday and Saturday 12pm to 11pm
An Edinburgh institution – Khushi's is one of Edinburgh's favourite Indian restaurants. When their previous restaurant on Victoria Street burnt down, they were out of action for sometime, but have set-up shop at the top of Leith Walk. It gets very busy in the evenings, with high demands for table, demonstrating just how good the food is.

Coffee and cheap eats

Punjab'n De Rasoi Café
122-124 Leith Walk, 07865 895 022

Wednesday to Saturday 11am to 4pm.

This Punjabi café on Leith Walk is run by the women of Sikh Sanjog, a charitable group that empowers Sikh and ethnic minority women, and gives them a place to go for support and advice. The café has a home- cooked feel, serving up traditional Punjabi curry, roti and lassi. Madhur Jaffrey even featured their recipes in her Curry Nation book and documentary on community cafes across the UK. They offer cookery classes on Monday and Tuesdays, 11am-1pm and 6pm to 8pm.

Café Casablanca

373 Leith Walk, 0131 629 5281

Everyday 11am to 9pm

This Moroccan restaurant is BYOB and they serve good value couscous and lamb kofte tangine, Moroccan coffee, baklava and thickshakes that Gwyneth Paltrow would approve of – banana, almond, fig, date and cinnamon. If you want something a bit less exotic, they also serve up the humble baked potato with a range of fillings. It's also BYOB.

Gaia

32 Crighton Place, 0131 553 7333

Gaiadeliedinburgh.gov.uk

Monday to Friday 9am to 6pm, Saturday 9.30am to 6pm, Sunday 11am to 4pm

This Sicilian deli is owned by the Dragotta family who are originally from Palermo. They do a range of cured meats and cheeses, speciality items to take away as well as traditional prepared food, soups and sandwiches to take-away or eat-in.

Yellow Bench

31 Crighton Place, 07510 851 842, yellowbench.edinburgh@gmail.com

www.yellowbench.co.uk

Every day 12pm to 9pm

This Polish cafe gets its name from the cheery bright yellow bench parked right outside. Their speciality is the crepes, in sweet or savoury style, there are traditional Polish main courses including pork in bread cumbs, potato salad, stroganoff, sauerkraut and dumplings.

Los Cardos

281 Leith Walk, 01341 555 6619, loscardosUK@gmail.com

www.loscardos.co.uk

Sunday to Thursday 12pm to 9pm, Friday and Saturday 12pm to 10pm

A take-away that does made to measure Tex-Mex food first inspired by a trip to Colorado. Taco Bell may be big in the States, but it's not that common in the UK, so this has a certain novelty value. You can choose your type of tortilla, choice of filling (which includes their signature MacSween's Haggis – for a Scotland meets Mexico experience) plus extra toppings, all for a good value £6.

Vinyl Villains

Shops

Storries Home Bakery
279 Leith Walk, 07973 215 534
Opening times vary
Get your bakery fix late at night, with some of the best meat pies, Classic Scottish bakery with all the traditional stuff - fruit slices (fly cemetery), empire biscuits, millionaire shortbread. Fudge donuts. This was how bakeries were in the 80s, and all for 50p.

Elvis Shakespeare
347 Leith Walk, 0131 561 1363
www.elvisshakespeare.com

Elvis Shakespeare has that nice, musty second hand shop smell, with rare books and second-hand records. They specialise in selling punk, alternative, indy and dance vinyl, as well as buying collections, and they also stock some DVD and fanzines. You can browse their collection on the website.

Valvona and Crolla Delicatessan and Caffe Bar
19 Elm Row, 0131 556 6066, sales@valvonacrolla.co.uk
www.valvonacrolla.co.uk
Monday to Thursday 8.30am to 6pm, Friday to Saturday 8am to 6.30pm, Sunday 10.30am to 4pm
A favourite of Nigella Lawson's, Valvona and Crolla has been selling Italian goodies to Edinburgh since 1934, originally as a stall for the small Italian immigrant community. With shelves stacked high with dry goods, a deli counter filled with Italian sausage, cured meats and cheese, Valvona and Crolla has become a bi-word for the tastes of middle-class Edinburgh. They have a restaurant in expensive Multrees Walk, but this deli has a rougher edge for being located on Leith Walk.

Vinyl Villains
5 Elm Row, 0131 558 1170, vinylvillains@elmrow.fsnet.co.uk
www.vinylvillainsrecords.co.uk

Going since 1983 as an independent record store, Vinyl Villians specialises in collectable records for buying and selling. They do original vinyl for hip-hop, folk, punk, rock, metal, jazz and blues, cult t-shirts, CDs, picture disks and 7 inch singles. It's the perfect place for wiling away some time in an old-school record shop.

Nicolson Street at night

SOUTHSIDE

Edinburgh's southside is student central, especially around George Square and Edinburgh University campus. Nicolson Street, which turns into Clerk Street, is the busy arterial rout, and it's where you can get some cheap eats in one of the many ethnic restaurants along this stretch.

Southside is also central for cultural attractions. There's the glass-fronted festival theatre for ballet, theatre and musicals, Queen's Hall has a programme of music, and on Chambers Street is the National Museum of Scotland.

In August, Edinburgh University's George Square, Bristo Square and Potterow become hubs for the festival with beer gardens, food stalls and temporary venues set up. The Spiegeltent in George Square is always packed and bustling with people waiting for shows or having outdoors drinks, while the Udderbelly in Bristo Square is a giant cow shaped tent which comes out in August.

Things to see

Surgeon's Hall Museum has some wonderfully gruesome displays and interesting exhibitions on the history of medical science, for which Edinburgh was once a leader.

Summerhall, at 1 Summerhall Place, in the former veterinary medicine college, known as Dick Vet, is also a hub for the arts, with art installations, a café and bar and a very tall chimney which was used for incinerations.

The Meadows is a massive grassy area where, on a sunny day, everyone seems to come out to play. You can watch people tie a rope between two trees and practice slack-lining, kick a football, toss a Frisbee or sit down with some beers and a picnic or barbeque with one of the BBQ spots dotted about.

George Square and its leafy garden is central to Edinburgh University, you'll see lots of students milling about during term time, and during August it's taken over as a venue for the festival, with outdoor bars, food stalls and tents for shows.

The University of Edinburgh

The Brass Monkey

Drinks

The Peartree

34 West Nicolson Street, 0131 667 7533

www.pear-tree-house.co.uk

Sunday to Thursday 11am to 12pm, Friday and Saturday 11am to 1am

The Peartree would be a very run of the mill pub if it wasn't located in a storybook stone building decorated with fairylights, and with a beautiful, large beer garden and cobbled courtyard. During the festival it becomes a real hub for people gathering for an outdoor drink between shows. The building dates back to 1749 as a merchant's house and the pub The Blind Poet shares the same building. It gets its name from blind poet Thomas Blacklock in the late 18th century, who was visited by Robert Burns and Dr Johnson. So there's some real, illustrious history in this building.

56 North

2-8 West Crosscauseway, 0131 662 8860, info@fiftysixnorth.co.uk

www.fiftysixnorth.co.uk

Every day 11am to 1am

A studenty bar with plenty of wooden tables and chairs on the pavement outside, décor of cask barrels, potted palms, cushioned seating and house music playing. They consider themselves a 'destination pub', and as well as selling a large range of cocktails, they also support local brewing by stocking Innis and Gunn and Stewart Brewing, and a large selection of Scottish gin.

The Meadows Bar

42 – 44 Buccleuch Street, 0131 667 6907

Monday to Friday 11am to 1am, Saturday and Sunday 12pm to 1am

This small pub, known as Moo Bar, for the pictures of cows that were on the walls, is an old-fashioned pub popular with academics and students and with some great atmosphere. The interior is very cosy, with couches to sink into and board games to play. The food menu is hearty, with a daily homemade pie, soup and pizza and a Mars Bar cream sundae for a calorific desert treat.

The Southern Bar

22-26 South Clerk Street, 0131 662 8926

www.thesouthern.co.uk

Sunday to Thursday 9am to 12am, Friday and Saturday 9am to 1am

Now one of the best bars down this stretch of South Clerk Street, The Southern Bar has been recently refurbished after being taken over by the Holyrood 9a crew, with dark green leather, red curtains and copper stools. They do an extensive burger menu including haggis burgers, venison burgers, lamb burgers and regular beef with an imaginative range of toppings and a choice of sweet potato fries, all served up on a wooden chopping board.

There's also an extensive selection of Scottish beers, and some European and US craft beers.

Brass Monkey
14 Drummond Street, 0131 556 1961
Monday to Saturday 11am to 1am, Sunday 12.30pm to 1am
One of the best loved pubs in Edinburgh by those in the know, The Brass Monkey's leather and wood space gets packed out, especially with the daily 3pm screenings of classic movies in the back room. It's got a traditional old man feel, cheapish drinks and with the addition of DJs and the culty film factor. In the movie room there are mattresses and cushions for complete relaxation, and a collage of iconic movie posters pasted up on the walls.

Summerhall Bar and Cafe
Summerhall Place, 0845 874 3000, info@summerhall.co.uk
www.summerhall.co.uk
Sunday to Thursday 12pm to 11pm, Friday and Saturday 12pm to 1am
In the former Dick Vet school, now an arts venue and creative space, the café features remnants from its veterinary studies days including jars of specimens, skeletons on the wall, adjustable operation tables with eclectic pieces and antique furniture. They stock Edinburgh's own Barney's Beer, which is brewed right on the spot of the original 18th century Summerhall brewery. As for food, they specialise in sharing plates, so you can dig in with a group of friends and try out a selection of meats, dips and crostini.

Field Restaurant. Photo Olga Tyukova

Restaurants

Mother India's Café

3 – 5 Infirmary Street, 0131 524 9801

www.motherindiascafeedinburgh.co.uk

Monday to Wednesday 12pm to 2pm, 5pm to 10.30pm, Thursday 12pm to 10.30pm, Friday and Saturday 12pm to 11pm, Sunday 12pm to 10pm

A 'Twist on Tapas' is how they describe their offerings at this Indian restaurant, from the owners of the famed Mother India in Glasgow's West End. It's a great way to sample lots of different, authentic dishes, mopped up with some naan bread and rice. They also do a take-away service.

Nawroz

26-30 Potterow, 0131 667 2299

www.nawrozrestaurant.com

Monday to Sunday 12pm to 11pm

This spacious, sleek Kurdish and Middle Eastern restaurant is very popular with students from the university campus across the road. The prices are good value, with a shawarma menu, charcoal grill, and plenty of vegetarian options involving chickpea, aubergine and okra. The huge front windows open up onto the pavement, adding even more space and you'll see some people kicking back after their lectures on a shisha pipe.

Nile Valley
6 Chapel Street, 0131 667 8200
Monday to Saturday 10am to 10pm
A good value, friendly and intimate East African restaurant, BYOB with no corkage charge, and lots of options for dishes to share, many with a middle-eastern influence. It has an eclectic hippy feel, with the posters for nights out and a downstairs area decked out with a Moorish theme.

Brazilian Sensation
117 – 119 Buccleuch Street, 0131 667 0400
www.braziliansensation.co.uk
Monday to Saturday 12pm to 4pm, and 5pm to 10pm by appointment only. Closed Sunday. During August everyday 12pm to late.
One of the few South American restaurants in Edinburgh and you can't miss it, as the outside is painted up the colours of a Brazilian flag. They have a vibrant blue and yellow interior and the menu is suitably exotic. Their lunch menu offers Brazilian snacks such as pão de queijo, bolinho de bacalhau, and coxinha, and tropical juices and smoothies. It opens in the evenings by reservation only.

Field Restaurant
41 West Nicolson Street, 0131 667 7010
www.fieldrestaurant.co.uk
Tuesday to Saturday 12pm to 2pm, 5.30pm to 9pm
One of Edinburgh's newest restaurants, Field has an intimate living room, farm feel with a mantelpiece decorated with little pigs, and a huge canvas of a cow on the walls. Owned by Rachel and Richard Conway and chef Gordon Craig from the Plumed Horse, they celebrate local and seasonal Scottish food. Game is from Braehead, fish from Newhaven, cheese from Ian Mellis, and they do a modern Scottish menu with bold flavour combinations. Pea panna

cotta is served with fried hamhock balls, maple-glazed duck and a popular chorizo burger with sweet potato fries, while Richard makes a different cheesecake every day. They also use Scottish wine suppliers and proudly keep the more expensive bottles affordable.

Celadon Thai Restaurant
49-51 Causewayside, 0131 667 1110
www.celadonrestaurant.co.uk
12 to 2.30pm Tuesday to Saturday, 5.30pm to 10.30pm Monday to Sunday
A serene setting for authentic Thai food, with rustic exposed stone walls, pictures of Buddha and simplistic but traditional decoration. Their menu included Thai favourites of green curry and red curry, Massaman lamb, and pad Thai, as well as fragrant dishes including Weeping Tiger, which is sliced chargrilled sirloin steak with fresh mint leaves, coriander, chilli and lime dressing, a warm salad of poached king scallop, mango and cashew nut.

Hanedan Restaurant
41 West Preston Street, 0131 667 4242
www.hanedan.co.uk
Tuesday to Sunday 12pm to 3pm and 5.30pm to late, closed Monday
A very popular Turkish restaurant that serves up speedy and hearty food. Because of the small space it has an intimate, chaotic taverna feel and the owner, a former chef in the Turkish army, adds some character to the place. Starters can be shared and come with olives and baskets of warmed pita bread, and main courses include filling mixed grill plates, meatballs and moussaka.

Mosque Kitchen
33 Nicolson Street, 0131 667 4035
Mosquekitchen.com
Everyday 11.30am to 11pm (closed Friday 12.50pm to 1.50pm for prayer)
This restaurant, run by the local Central Mosque, offers very good value Pakistani cooking, with a choice of three vegetable curry and rice for £5, a meat curry and rice for £4, and samosa, naan breads and kebabs. There's an interesting mix of hippy students, homeless people and tourists gathered inside, and the interior is big, sparse and clean.

Spoon on Nicolson Street

Peter's Yard ,near The Meadows

Coffee and cheap eats

Himalayan Centre and Vegetarian Café
20 South Clerk Street, 0131 662 9818, himalayashop@hotmail.com
If you like Nepal, then this is the place to come. Suitably The Himalayan Centre was opened after the owner had a chance meeting with the Dalai Lama at the Scottish Parliament in 2005. With the feel of a new-agey, backpacker café in the Himalayas, the centre sells hand-made goods such as jewellery and wall-hangings from India and Nepal and Tibet, and a café that serves masala chai, (apparently the best in Edinburgh), the perennial backpacker favourite of banana pancakes, a daily vegetarian curry and a 'love' cake. They also do treatments such as reiki, tui na massage, meditation and yoga.

Black Medicine Coffee
2 Nicolson Street, 0131 557 6269
www.blackmed.co.uk
Monday to Saturday 8am to 8pm, Sunday 9am to 8pm
A Native American theme for this cool café, with a stonewall interior, totem pole, carved wooden seats and a shelf full of apothecary bottles. This is the original branch, which has spawned two more on the southside, on 108 Marchmont Road and by The Meadows, at 7 Barclay Terrace. As well as homemade cakes they have a good Panini selection, ham and brie croissants and a free Tunnock's teacake or banana with every large coffee.

Red-Box Noodle Bar
51-53 West Nicolson Street, 0131 662 0828
www.red-boxnoodlebar.co.uk
Everyday 12pm to 10pm
Another very popular place with students, Red Box noodle bar specialises in take-away noodle boxes, as the name suggests. For £5.40, you pick a combination from a choice of noodles, meat, vegetables and stir fry sauce, and served up in one of those New York-style take away cartons.

Engine Shed Café
19 St Leonard's Lane, 0131 662 0040

Monday to Saturday 10am to 4pm

For those who want to give something back, then the Engine Shed is a great place to support as it employs people with learning difficulties to give them experience in a work environment, and follows the principles of Rudolf Steiner. They bake delicious, freshly-baked bread and run a café in a 19th century building originally owned by British Rail.

Spoon

6a Nicolson Street, 0131 623 1752

www.spoonedinburgh.co.uk

Monday to Saturday 10am to 10pm, Sunday 12pm to 5pm

In the space formerly known as the Nicolson Café, this is where JK Rowling, as an impoverished writer, penned the first Harry Potter novel. It's in a big, spacious room on an upper-floor with eclectic retro furnishings and an old-world traveller vibe to the décor with world maps embellished on tables, old mirrors and chintzy china. They serve more than just coffee and cake, as they serve up sophisticated dishes in a relaxed setting.

Peckhams Deli and Café

49 South Clerk Street, 0131 668 3737

www.peckhams.co.uk

Monday to Saturday 8am to 10pm, Sunday 9am to 10pm

An unfortunate victim of the recession, Peckham's, one of Scotland's leading independent food shops for several decades, had to shut down two of their shops in Edinburgh, but their branch on the southside is still going strong. It's kept in high regard by a discerning group of customers with its selection of luxury dry goods, baskets of bread, organic wines and beer, a deli serving cured meats, cheese, quiche, salads and cakes, and a café to enjoy it all right there on the spot.

Beanscene

99 Nicolson Street, 0131 667 5697, info@beanscene.com

www.beanscene.co.uk

Monday to Saturday 8am to 10pm, Sunday 9am to 10pm

A coffee chain Beanscene may be, but it's a Scottish one, and a successful one at that, popular with students and cool southsiders who like the local feel combined with the hip 60s coffee bars of San Francisco and Greenwich Village. They pride themselves of their eclectic music taste, with live gigs by local musicians, and they also do BYOB.

10 to 10 in Delhi
67 Nicolson Street, 07536 757 770, bookings@10to10indelhi.com
www.10to10indelhi.com
Monday to Saturday 10am to 10pm, Sunday 12pm to 10pm
With its India backpacker café interior, and cheap prices to match, 10 to 10 in Delhi has a relaxed, young vibe and colourful décor. Lead chef Alieu cooks up a student menu of tasty curries, roti filled with chicken masala or aloo palak, chatpatti, soup with naan bread, samosa and a mixed plate for £5.95, which can be washed down with tropical fruit juice or a mango lassi.

Peter's Yard Coffee House and Bakery
Quartermile, 27 Simpson Loan, 0131 228 5876, info@petersyard.com
www.petersyard.com
Monday to Friday 7.30am to 7pm, Saturday and Sunday 9am to 7pm
This contemporary Swedish artisan bakery in a glassy, spacious new development by the Meadows is always busy with a bustling turn-out of Edinburgh uni students, nearby workers and those making the commute through the Meadows. They specialise in Swedish sourdough crispbread, and there are baskets stacked with breads and cookies, and long benches to share, as part of their Swedish ethos of taking time to share food and conversation with old and new friends. There's also a take-away coffee and ice-cream place just round the corner in similar modernist building.

Shops

Apple Jack
37 South Bridge, 0131 556 5324
Monday to Saturday 10am to 6pm, Sunday 12pm to 5pm

Apple Jack is a funky clothes shop, head shop and piercing parlour. They sell comic book patterned dresses, hoodies, logo t-shirts, funky paints and nail polishes, stud bracelets and jewellery, all to help you realise your inner emo. As a head shop they sell smoking paraphernalia and a large selection of bongs.

Forbidden Planet
40 – 41 South Bridge Street, 0131 558 8226
www.forbiddenplanet.co.uk
Monday to Friday 10am to 5.30pm, Saturday 10am to 4.30pm, closed Sunday
Forbidden Planet is one of Scotland's biggest and best comic book stores with a huge selection of comics, graphic novels and merchandise, as well as a range of cult toys and action figures from Star Wars, James Bond and Doctor Who. If you want to pick up a model Dalek, a Game of Thrones T-shirt or a rare Mark Morrison graphic novel then this should be your first stop.

Choco-latte
39 South Clerk Street, 0131 667 0091
www.choco-latte.co.uk
This deceptively small Willy Wonka style chocolate shop is a paradise of tooth-decaying riches, with sweets stacked up on shelves and in the window. They sell mega-sized muffins decorated with Mars Bar, Oreo and Maltesers, slabs of tray-bake, hand-made chocolates, mounds of playground sweets including cola bottles and flying saucers, and that classic Scottish treat, tablet.

Blackwell's Bookshop
53 – 59 South Bridge, 0131 622 8222
Monday 9am to 5pm, Tuesday 12pm to 6pm, Wednesday and Thursday 9am to 6pm, Friday 9am to 6.30pm, Saturday 9am to 4pm, Sunday 12pm to 6pm
The place to come for academic and school books due to its proximity to the university, this branch of Blackwell is built up on several floors, and has a maze of different rooms and staircases to explore. They also have a large travel department, a great selection of children's books and anything else you are looking for.

Till's Bookshop

1 Hope Park Crescent, 0131 667 0895, tillsbookshop@btconnect.com

www.tillsbookshop.co.uk

Monday to Friday 12pm to 7.30pm, Saturday 11pm to 6pm, Sunday 12pm to 5.30pm

If there was ever a quirky but traditional-looking bookshop needed for a sitcom or a romantic comedy, then Till's Bookshop would be the place to go. It's in a beautiful, quiet location overlooking the Meadows, with ceiling-high bookshelves, a range of first editions and rare books at reasonable prices, as well as a film memorabilia collection of original movie posters and lobby cards. Ian Rankin even paid a visit once to film a BBC programme.

Casa Morada

89 Causewayside, 0131 667 7060, info@casamorada.co.uk

www.casamorada.co.uk

Monday to Saturday (closed on Tuesdays) 10am to 5pm, Sunday 12pm to 4pm

If you are wandering down Causewayside, then stylish Casa Morada is worth a look, for their ever changing display of quirky and bizarre interior decorations and furniture. Some of the items could include a stags head and angel wings hanging from the wall.

Love Hate Tattoo

59-61 Newington Road, 0131 667 6780, info@lovehatetattoo.co.uk

www.lovehatetattoo.co.uk

Tuesday to Saturday 11am to 7pm

Considered one of the best tattoo parlours in the city if not the UK, Love Hate is a clean, spacious family run parlour which has even been endorsed by TV show Miami Ink. They have guest artists who specialise in particular styles. Their renowned artists, including Flo Nuttall, create intricate designs of pin-up girls, skulls and animals, and people do travel across the country to get inked at Love Hate.

A police box turned coffee bar

MORNINGSIDE, BRUNTSFIELD AND MARCHMONT

Morningside is Edinburgh's area of well-to-do gentility, but summarised by the expression "all fur coat and nae knickers." It's an exclusive area of residential streets with large Victorian villas and expansive gardens.

The famous Morningside accent has been sent up by many comics, especially Perrier award-winning Simon Fanshawe who made his trade in comparing Glasgow's Kelvinside with Morningside. "Kelvinside is a much harsher sound and much more showy. Morningside is about not telling people the truth. It's the wink and the nod," he has said.

Muriel Spark's Miss Jean Brodie is the classic Morningside lady – elegant, aloof, cultured, pursed lips in disapproval. As well as being home of JK Rowling and Ian Rankin, Morningside was also the birthplace of Maisie, the illustrated cat in the books by Aileen Paterson, and the home of Isabel Dalhousie from Alexander McCall Smith's series of books.

Morningside turns into Bruntsfield, lively and a popular place for student living in the tenement flats that make up the area. Marchmont is the quiet area south of the Meadows, again a popular place for student flat-sharing and artistic types.

Things to see

One of the highlights of the area is the family owned Dominion Cinema – a proper, old style art moderne cinema that has been given a make-over, with big comfy sofas to watch films on while kicking back with a glass of wine.

The Morningside Clock was once in the middle of the road and was part of Morningside Station which closed in 1962, as Edinburgh's railway line shut down. The entrance is where the RBS branch is now.

Holy Corner gets its name from the number of churches on each corner – there used to be four, but now three remain. Morningside North Parish Church is now The Eric Liddell centre, a community centre named after the Olympic athlete whose story the film Chariots of Fire was based on.

The Hermitage of Braid and Blackford Hill, just south of Morningside is a quiet retreat for woodland walking, wildlife observing and views over the city. See the outdoors chapter for more info.

Drinks

The Canny Man's Pub
237 Morningside Road, 0131 447 1484
Monday to Sunday 12pm to 11pm
This charming old pub dating back to 1871 has a lot of history contained within its rooms. Stacked up on shelves, and hung up on the walls are old books, clocks, moose heads and antiques. It also has a reputation for being quite snobby - rude bartenders can sometimes enforce the smart but casual dress code, and the no mobile phones and no backpacker rules.

Restaurants

Caffe e Cucina
372 Morningside Road, 0131 447 0345
caffecucinaedinburgh.co.uk
Monday to Friday 10am to 11pm, Saturday 10.15am to 10.30pm, Sunday 10.15am to 10pm
This authentically Italian restaurant, more sophisticated Milan than bustling Rome, has a muted, minimal interior with newsprint seat covers and metropolis wallpaper. Food is all prepared by Italian chefs behind a bustling counter, the food is uses fresh, tasty ingredients, fresh Italian puddings like tiramisu, and the gigantic man-size calzone is something to behold. The Italian proprietor operates the coffee machine, and the espresso is rich and strong.

Montpeliers Bar and Brasserie
159-161 Bruntsfield Place, 0131 229 3115
Seven days 9am to 1am
www.montpeliersedinburgh.co.uk
This Bruntsfield institution has a lively bar area and warm, atmospheric restaurant section. Recline on one of their chesterfield leather sofas by candlelight, or sit outside with a glass of wine on a summer's evening. While it has a French bistro feel, the menu is more eclectic with Thai and Italian influences. Also look out for their deals for a tenner – two main courses at lunchtime or a starter and maincourse at dinner.

Coffee and cheap eats

Henri of Edinburgh
376 Morningside Road, 0131 447 8877
Monday to Friday 8.30am to 6pm, Saturday 8.30pm to 5.30pm, Sunday 9am to 3.30pm
A French bistro and deli with that pungent cheese smell, jars of French produce, mustards, haricots, macaroons from Paris, and fresh breads that sell out quickly. They also have a branch in Stockbridge, at 48 Raeburn Place.

The Zulu Lounge
366 Morningside Road, 0131 466 8337
Monday to Friday 7.30am to 6pm, Saturday and Sunday 8am to 5pm.
A very busy little café with a stripy zebra shop front and some African fabric detail inside, and appropriately enough across the road from Nile Street. Their Zulu milkshakes have a crazy amount of options to create your own milkshake (chocolate, crunchie flavor with toffee popcorn topping for example). They also do toasties, bagels, foot long gatzbys, and rich homemade muffins. There are only a few seats by the window, so it becomes a bit of a squeeze.

S Luca Ice-cream parlour
16 Morningside Road, 0131 446 0233
www.s-luca.o.uk

Seven days, 9am to 10pm

This family-run ice-cream business from Musselburgh, the sea-side town just outside of Edinburgh, has a reputation for making the finest ice-cream in Edinburgh, and has manufactured since 1908. Luca Scappaticcio was an immigrant from Casino in Italy who became a pastry chef at the Balmoral Hotel. He and wife Anastasia rented a shop in Musselburgh, and before the days of freezers, kept their ice-cream cold with dry ice. Their Morningside parlour in an old stone building next to a church, now sells Jaffa Cake ice-cream and Irn Bru sorbet alongside the more traditional flavours.

Falko (Konditormeister)
185 Bruntsfield Place, 0131 656 0763
www.falko.co.uk
Closed Monday and Tuesday, Wednesday to Saturday 9am to 6pm, Sunday 9.30am to 6pm.
This authentically German bakery with its wrought iron entrance way, a dark mahogany interior, and shelves stacked with German breads, is a favourite for coffee and sachertorte in Bruntsfield. The cakes and gateau are faithful to their country of origin, with marzipan is shipped from Lubeck, there's a large selection of German tea and they also do healthy salads and sandwiches for lunch.

The Chocolate Tree
123 Bruntsfield Place, 0131 228 3144
Monday to Saturday 8am to 8pm, Sunday 9am to 8pm
www.the-chocolate-tree.co.uk
Inspired by thick hot chocolate from Barcelona, The Chocolate Tree was one of the first places in the UK to makes chocolate from the bean. They serve up gelato, cakes, café gelato and milkshakes, macaroons, and cloudy lemonade, under the watchful eye of a painting of the Sistine Chapel. They also serve a large range of Chocolate Tree organic chocolate bars.

Loopy Lorna's Tea House
Church Hill Theatre, 33a Morningside Road, 0131 447 3042, bookings@loopylornas.com
www.loopylornas.com

Monday to Sunday 10am to 5pm
A real Scottish tearoom in the basement of the Church Hill Theatre which has been named the best independent eatery in Scotland and given the Tea Guild Award of Excellence. It's named in tribute to 'loopy Lorna', the late Liverpudlian mother of the owner. They have teas blended by a world expert, freshly baked scones, and a homemade cake experience using family and traditional recipes.

Shops

Bakery Andante
352 Morningside Road, 0131 447 8473
Monday to Saturday 7.30am to 6pm, Sunday 8.30am to 1pm
A clean white, airy bakery with trays of delicious slices in the window of bakewell, lemon frangipani, sourdough, brownies, and croissants all baked in the kitchen in the back. The artisan breads are proudly cooked slowly so as to avoid the use of added baker's yeast raising agents and other chemicals. Baker Jon Wood's sourdough has won the Great Taste gold award, and the Covenanter's loaf is inspired by the Pentland Hills.

Calzeat
412 Morningside Road, 0131 446 9353
www.calzeat.com
Monday to Sunday 11.30am to 4.30pm, closed Wednesday
Calzeat are creators and innovators of fine Scottish fabric as designed by Fiona Knight. Calzeat has collaborated with young and upcoming Scottish designers including Obscure Couture and Hayley Scanlan and have displayed their works during New York tartan week. They sell Celtic throws, jacquard, scarves made from Borders lambs wool and products weaved with computer aided design systems.

SH jewellery
98 Morningside Road, 0131 447 5544
www.shjgallery.com
Monday to Saturday 10.30am to 5.30pm, Sunday by appointment

Opened in 2011 by silversmith Sarah Hutchison, SH jewellery showcases her own designs as well as silver jewellery from other selected designers. Sarah incorporates precious stones into her designs, which are heavily textured and influenced by nature, and a range of rings inspired by growth into decay.

Morningside Gallery

94 Morningside Road, 0131 447 3041

www.morningsidegallery.co.uk

Monday to Saturday 10am to 6pm, closed Sunday

This sleek gallery showcases the work of Scottish artists, some well known, some up and coming. Past works on display includes Lynn Rodgie's paintings of Edinburgh street scenes that look like Paris, haunted landscapes by Elaine Cunningham and moody oil paintings by Gordon Wilson. Sculpture and glass are also on display.

Fifi Wilson

181 Bruntsfield Place, 0131 228 2929

Monday to Saturday 10pm to 6pm, Sunday 12pm to 5pm

The Scottish outpost for the funky London boutique, selling unique designer labels and fun designs by Sonia Rykiel, Bella Fraud and Laundry Industry. The shop is a haven of colourful, quirky patterned and beautiful pieces for the "independent, hard-working, fun busy woman."

Miss Dixie Bell

19 Bruntsfield Place, 0131 629 7783, info@missdixiebelle.co.uk

www.missdixiebelle.co.uk

Monday to Saturday 10.30am to 5.30pm, Sunday 12pm to 4pm

A stylish burlesque boutique with chandeliers and chi-chi wallpaper, which not only sells vintage-style dresses, corsets, What Katie Did bras and other pin-up pieces, but they can also do hair and make-up in their downstairs studio, for a complete transformation. Prices are around £40 for either hair or make-up. So you can style yourself into a 1940s siren with hair in a pompadour, or a 50s sex-pot a la Jayne Mansfield.

Bohemia

17 Roseneath Street, 0131 478 9609

www.bohemiadesign.co.uk

Monday to Saturday 10am to 6pm, Sunday 1pm to 5pm

Bohemia sells beautiful, unique products selected by a team from all corners of the world. They sell cards and wrapping paper, stylish clothes by Vero Moda and Sugarhill, leather footstools, owl cushions, purses and bags.

Photo C Young

Tollcross and Lothian Road

Tollcross is lively and a little bit seedy, with lots of pubs, cafes and independent boutiques, and popular for its close approximation to the Meadows. Lothian Road can get raucous late at night, drunken fights spilling out onto the streets, and there also several stripclubs and 'saunas' – the euphemism for brothels, which are almost tolerated by the Police in this city.

Lothian and Road and Tollcross have an inordinate number of venues for live bands, cinemas, theatre, performance and comedy. There's the Traverse Theatre, The Usher Hall, The Picturehouse for live music, and cinemas The

Odeon, the Cameo and The Filmhouse. (See the cinema section for more details.) The big screen at Festival Square shows Wimbledon matches, important sporting events, and Royal celebrations.

The Blackbird's orange bicycle, photo courtesy The Blackbird

Bennet's Bar, photo C Young

Drinks

Bennet's Bar
8 Leven Street, 0131 229 5143
www.bennetsbar.co.uk
Everyday 11am to 11pm
This historic bar, kept in a 1906 time warp with its original features still in place, was popular as a post-theatre drinking hole with the actors from The King's Theatre opposite. It's often used with film companies scouting for an authentic bar, with mahogany panelling that holds 150 different single malt Scotch whiskeys behind the bar, the taps for adding water to whisky, Grecian-inspired framing around the mirrors and a separate booth where the ladies would drink, keeping them separated from the men.

Lebowski's Bar Edinburgh
18 Morrison Street, 0131 466 1779, info@lebowskis.co.uk
www.lebowskis.co.uk
Monday to Sunday 12pm to 1am
Lebowski's takes its name from the Coen Brothers film, and pays tribute in a big way, with a White Russian menu dedicated to characters from the film and with quotes to illustrate the point. You almost expect the wait staff to come out in dressing gowns to take your order. They do an interesting 'perfect serve' - Innis and Gunn with Scottish fudge, Gaorunn gin and apple juice with slice apple and tonic, and Laphroaig whisky with Scottish blue cheese and Aaron oatcakes. The succulent burgers will also go down a treat. As they say, always trust the bartender, and the Dude.

The Blackbird
37-39 Leven Street, 0131 228 2280
www.theblackbridedinburgh.co.uk
Monday to Sunday 10am to 1am
With its bright orange bicycle hanging up over the dark grey exterior, The Blackbird is a super trendy new locale owned by the same team as Hamilton's and Treacle in the New Town. They have taken over an old man's drinking hole and turned it into a hip bar with a stripped back interior and enhanced

original features such as the fireplaces. Add in a leather sofa and candle-light interior, chatter around the busy bar, hot staff, a food menu printed on grease-proof paper and a new beer garden.

Cameo Cinema Bar

38 Home Street, 0871 902 5723

Part of the Cameo cinema, but with an entrance round the corner, the Cameo is a popular bar for bearded students and artsy types. The bar has an art deco style front, and a wall covered in film stills from decades' worth of movies, which makes a fun game guessing where they are from. They also have a range of snacks including soups, paninis and brownies. Filmgoers can get their serves of wine or beer in a plastic cup and take it in to sip while watching a movie.

Henrick's Bar and Bistro

1 – 3 Barclay Place, 0131 229 2442, info@henricksbar.com

www.henricksbar.com

Everyday 10am to 1am

A cross between a bar and a bistro, Henrick's has a steady stream of customers and friendly staff who serve drinks by table service, and at night time the muted interior is lit by the glow of candlelight. There's a tiny little patio area out back, although any sunshine is blocked by the high stone walls. There's a good value £10.95 pre-theatre menu, ideal for the King's Theatre across the road. They also pride themselves on their wine list and hold wine tastings and guest appearances from wine experts on the first Monday evening of the month.

The Hanging Bat Beer Cafe

133 Lothian Road, 0131 229 0759, beer@thehangingbat.com

www.thehangingbat.com

Sunday to Thursday 12pm to 12am, Friday and Saturday 12pm to 1am

The Hanging Bat is an ultra trendy bar for beer and BBQ with a wood and exposed stone interior – a stripped wood bar, strips of wood on the wall and wooden floorboards. Casks of home-brew are kept cool in the fridge behind the bar. They can organise brewing and tasting events in which you get to make (sensible) suggestions on the ingredients for your own beer. There's a selection of 20 cask and keg beers on tap around 100 bottle beers, and food consists of hot dogs, barbeque and cakes supplied by local café Love Crumbs.

The Earl of Marchmont
22 Marchmont Crescent, 0131 662 1877
Theearlofmarchmont.blogspot.com
Monday to Saturday 12pm to 1am, Sunday 12pm to 12am
This is *the* local pub in Marchmont, with a sophisticated group of customers, from students to professionals, and loyal regulars. It has a traditional pub feel, but with eclectic touches such as a glitzy chandelier, and seating on the pavement outside to observe the Marchmont people go by.

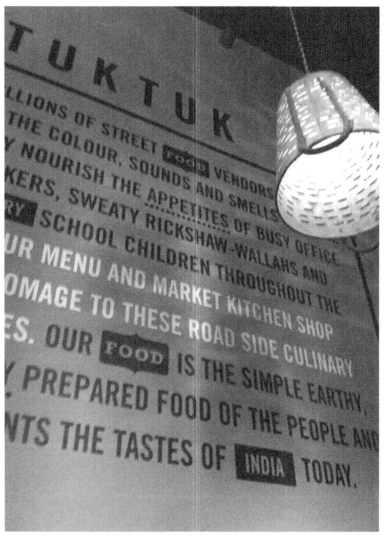

Tuk Tuk Indian Street Food

Restaurants

Tuk Tuk Indian Street Food
1 Leven Street, 0131 228 3322
Monday to Sunday 12pm to 10.30pm
www.tuktukonline.com
Creating the effect of being transported to Mumbai railway station or on a train heading to Delhi, Tuk Tuk creates the type of Indian food served on the roadside or as railway dishes. With Bengali music on the stereo, an orange and grey colour scheme, and an industrial-feel, especially in the toilets, this is an Indian restaurant with a difference.

The Apartment Bistro
7 – 13 Barclay Place, 0131 228 6456, theapartmenthq@hotmail.co.uk
www.apartmentrestaurant.com
Everyday 12pm to 10pm (Friday and Saturday open until 10.30pm)
With a stylish modern floor and glass doors that slide open on a sunny day, The Apartment is a good option for a relaxed yet formal lunch and dinner with an intimate feel. Mains are around the £15 mark, with choices such as roasted venison and beetroot rosti, pan-seared duck breast, hake fillet or roasted chicken and king prawns with mango and chilli salsa.

Piatto Verde
7 Dundee Terrace, 0131 228 2588
Tuesday to Thursday and Sunday 5pm to 11pm, Friday and Saturday 5pm to 12am, closed Monday
If you are going to see a film at Fountainpark, then instead of chain pub food, try this cosy little Italian restaurant nearby, with its nice, simple rustic décor. Creamy risotto, rich parmigiana di melenzane, bruschetta, crisp pizzas, fresh mozzarella with tomato, basil and olive oil, a classic tiramisu to finish, and all with the home cooked feel, and an intimate, candle-lit atmosphere and charming staff. reet

Kampung Ali
97 – 101 Fountainbridge, 0131 228 5069
www.kampungali.com
Monday to Thursday 12pm to 2.30pm, 5pm to 11pm, Friday, Saturday and
Sunday 12pm to 11pm
A supremely popular Malaysian restaurant serving up authentic dishes,
Kampung Ali has the feel of a Kuala Lumpur canteena, with a menu of
pictures, rows of tables and a big emblazoned KL nightscape on the wall.
Chef and owner Mr Lee, originally from Negeri Sembilan, had previous restaurants in Malaysia. There's moreish Roti cenai, Malaysian satay, rendang
beef, curry laksa noodle and nasi Gerang, and some wonderfully weird drink/
deserts pearl milk tea.

Coffee and cheap eats

Made in France
5 Lochrin Place, 0131 221 1184
Monday to Friday 10am to 6pm, Saturday 10am to 4pm, closed Sunday
This friendly little French café has an eclectic Parisian style interior, with
home-made pastries and a menu of croquet monsieur, fondue, and strawberry
pound cake. You can also phone up and order a tasty hamper for enjoying in
the Meadows.

The Forest Café
141 Lauriston Place, 0131 229 4922
Blog.theforest.org.uk
Monday to Sunday 10am to 11pm
The Forest vegetarian café is a not for profit gathering space for creative types
with a vision for the arts. It's pretty much staffed by volunteers who have a
passion for what the Forest stands for. There's a sense of everything being
recycled, from the furniture to the graffiti-covered concrete walls, odd mugs
for coffee and mismatched cutlery. The food is wholesome, cheap and the
atmosphere is friendly. There are also different events such as drama workshops, Monday film night, local musicians and local art work on display.

Meadowberry frozen yoghurt

10 Barclay Terrace, 07592 147 362, info@meadowberry.co.uk

www.meadowberry.co.uk

Jumping on the fro-yo craze, Meadowberry serves fat free or low fat frozen yoghurt with a choice of toppings such as fresh fruit, nuts or jellybeans, and the option for having it in a cup or cone, inside or on the go.

Toast

146 Marchmont Road, 0131 446 9873

www.toastedinburgh.co.uk

Monday to Saturday 10am to 10pm, Sunday 10am to 5pm

Beside a charming old lane with gas lamps, Toast is a place for breakfast and brunches, but they also do lunch and dinner. The weekend brunch has everything you could hope for – full Scottish breakfast with black pudding and tatty scone, French toast with bananas, caramel and crème fraiche, perhaps the reason why people jostle for a table. Lunch and dinner has a range of Scottish inspired dishes with some Asian and Mediterranean influence.

Shops

Lupe Pintos

24 Leven Street, 0131 228 6241

Lupepintos.com

Monday to Wednesday and Saturday 10am to 6pm, Thursday and Friday 10am to 7pm, Sunday 12.30pm to 5.30pm

A shop specialising in imported products from Mexico, Spain and America, Lupe Pinto shelves are stacked high with goodies for baking and cooking, as well as drinking. They have supplies of different hot sauces, Mexican chocolate for making mole, 100% agave tequila, and Spanish favourites, as well as advice on recipes for cooking up a feast. And if you want to try your own authentic American pancakes or need corn syrup for a recipe, then they have it covered.

CAROLINE YOUNG

Totty Rocks

45 – 47 Barclay Place, 0131 229 0474, mail@tottyrocks.com

www.tottyrocks.com

A gorgeous, unique boutique with every item designed by fashion duo Lynsey Blackburn and Holly Mitchell. The layout is funky and fresh with striking red and white décor, horse and hound wallpaper and pictures on the wall, and the clothes on display are forward-thinking and angular shapes, structured, striped tops, quirky printed dresses and cool hats.

Newhaven Harbour

EXPLORING OUTSIDE THE CITY CENTRE

Newhaven

Newhaven was once an independent fishing village and still has the sense of its own history and traditions. Newhaven harbour has a 19th century lighthouse at its entrance and further back is the village with its cobbled road and rows of old fisherman cottages with steps leading up to the first floor.

The Newhaven fishwives had a reputation for beauty and industry, selling the fish from creels on their back, and dressed in distinctive striped dresses and headdresses. The fishing way of life was fascinating to Victorian photographers who captured the characters of the area, and their celebrations on Gala Day.

The huge Newhaven anchor, on the corner of Annfield Street, is a symbol of the rich history of Newhaven.

It's worth going for a walk by the harbour, with views out to Fife, and then maybe a pint in one of the local pubs.

The Starbank Inn
64 S Laverockbank Avenue, 0131 552 4141, starbankinn.edinburgh@belhavenpubs.net
www.starbankinn-edinburgh.co.uk
Monday to Wednesday 11am to 11pm, Thursday 11am to 12pm, Friday and Saturday 11am to 1am, Sunday 12pm to 11pm
Just beside Starbank Park, with its moon and star-shaped flower beds, The Starbank Inn is a traditional pub in a nice old stone building, and a local

THE COOL GUIDE TO EDINBURGH

favourite for a quick pint by the fireplace, or to enjoy some typical pub grub. It also has great views over the water.

The Harbour Inn
4 – 6 Fishmarket Square, 0131 552 3968
The oldest pub in Newhaven, it has that really traditional sense, with live music every now and again and a Monday evening cheese board. It's the type of place with traditional ales on tap, and plenty of locals around the bar chatting away with the staff.

Portobello

Portobello is Edinburgh' beach – only three miles from Edinburgh's city centre and was once the holiday destination for many Scots.

Porty is classic British seaside with its Mr Whippy ice cream, neon flashing arcade games and a windswept promenade. The wide sandy beach gets busy on a sunny day and there are also opportunities for water sports, swimming and kayaking, although the temperature of the sea is always brisk.

Porty also has a strong community spirit that keeps it local, with lots of independent shops, cafes and pubs, and a monthly market in Brighton Park.

Portobello Swim Centre
57 Promenade, Portobello, 0131 669 6888, info.psc@edinburghleisure.co.uk
www.edinburghleisure.co.uk/venues/portobello-swim-centre
A beautifully preserved Victorian swimming baths located right on the prom, which also has one of the only Turkish baths in Scotland.

The Espy
62 – 64 Bath Street, 0131 669 0082, the.espy.porty@gmail.com
Monday to Thursday 10am to 11pm, Friday to Sunday 10am to 1am

The Esplanade pub, known as The Espy, is the main social point of Portobello and has that real beachside bar feel to it with its location on the promenade and looking out to sea. They serve craft beers, home-made ginger beer, a menu with burgers and good breakfasts, DJs play at the weekend and they hold regular cinema nights.

The Beach House Cafe
57 Bath Street, 0131 657 2636
www.thebeachhousecafe.co.uk
Monday to Friday 9am to 5.30pm, Saturday and Sunday 9am to 6pm
With the vibe of an Aussie cafe, but with less sunshine, The Beach House cafe is a great place for some brunch, with tables and chairs right outside on the promenade to take in the sea air. They serve organic coffees, locally baked cakes, breads and scones and healthy soups and salads

Dalriada Bar
77 Promenade, 0131 454 4500, terrymagill@dalriabar.co.uk
Dalriadabar.co.uk
Monday to Thursday 12pm to 11pm, Friday to Saturday 12pm to 12pm
Funky Dalriada is a bar and live music venue, with Friday fireside sessions, a Saturday afternoon devoted to traditional folk music and on Saturday evenings they support up and coming bands from 9 to 12pm. It's in an impressive old building right on the prom, with a beer garden out front and a cosy interior, with a basic food menu and a good selection of cask beers.

Duddingston Village

The charming little village of Duddingston is on the east side of Holyrood Park, near Duddingston Loch, which was used for skating and curling centuries ago. In fact Henry Raeburn's painting, the Skating Minister was set on Duddingston Loch.

Duddingston Kirk, built in 1124 and on Old Church Lane, overlooks the loch, and at no.9 The Causeway, is where Bonnie Prince Charlie held a war meeting at before the Battle of Prestonpans in 1745.

Dr Neil's Garden is a peaceful retreat by the loch. It's open from 10am to dusk, with a request of a donation. With benches, stonemasonry, water features and a monkey-puzzle tree, it feels like a secret escape from the city.

But the highlight of Duddingston is the famous Sheep Heid Inn, once a haven for artists and writers.

The Sheep Heid Inn
43 – 45 The Causeway, 0131 661 7974
www.thesheepheidedinburgh.co.uk
Monday to Thursday 11am to 11pm, Friday and Saturday 11am to 12am, Sunday 12.30pm to 11pm
The Sheep Heid Inn, Edinburgh's oldest pub, located at the back of Arthur's Seat has been restored to maintain its picturesquely rustic charm and cosy old interior. You could imagine the horses being tied up outside as travellers took a break for an ale at the inn. But it's also a gastro-pub with good food, a selection of Scottish beers, there's a courtyard for outdoor drinking and an indoor bowling alley which can be booked out for parties.

CAROLINE YOUNG

The Cramond Inn, photo C Young

Cramond

Cramond may be a little twee, with its café and museum on the promenade, but it's a peaceful, quiet spot by the Forth, with a rocky beach, views all the way over to Fife and even Perthshire, and the walk over the causeway to Cramond Island (but remember to check the tides so you don't get stranded!)

The Cramond Inn
30 Cramond Glebe Road, Cramond Village, 0131 336 2035
Monday to Thursday 11am to 11pm, Friday ad Saturday 11am to 12am, Sunday 12.30pm to 11pm
A very picturesque pub in a B-listed former coaching inn, all white walled and original windows, with a dark, ye olde interior of antique furniture, and benches outside for soaking up the view over the Forth. As part of the Samuel Smith pub chain, the customer service in this pub has been criticised and the

food is not great, but if you are looking for a pub in this area, then choose it for scenery rather than service.

South Queensferry

South Queensferry is located down by the Forth, just between the Forth Rail Bridge and the Forth Road Bridge. It has a small harbour and an old high street, and has retained its own independence with the tradition of a gala day and the pagan Burry Man ritual once a year. There's also the Loony Dook, the ritual of jumping into the freezing Forth on New Year's day, but has become increasingly commercialised with a £6 charge.

Walking through Station Road Park, there is a new walkway and information points where you can get great views over to the Forth and the railway bridge.

Joyce Patton boutique
8 East Terrace, 0787 940 7336, joyce@joycepaton.com
Saturday and Sunday 11am to 6pm, or by appointment
An Alice in Wonderland of a boutique, Joyce Patton is a costume lover's paradise with custom-made corsets and hats, couture pieces and Harris Tweed dresses, gowns and jacket. Joyce Patton has been named accessories designer of the year at The Scottish Fashion Awards and has worked on major campaigns, including Ultimo.

The Hawes Inn
7 Newhalls Road, 0131 331 1990
www.vintageinn.co.uk/thehawesinnsouthqueensferry
Monday to Saturday 12pm to 11pm, Sunday 12pm to 10.30pm
The Hawes Inn is the oldest pub in Queensferry and was even mentioned in Robert Louis Stevenson's Kidnapped. It has outdoor tables with views to the Bridge, and a cosy old charm inside, with cask ales, a good selection of ciders and a good food menu.

The Grill at Dakota Forthbridge

11 Ferrymuir Retail Park, 0131 319 3690

www.dakotahotels.co.uk

Monday to Saturday 12pm to 2.30pm, 6 to 10.30pm, Sunday 1pm to 5pm, 6pm to 9pm

The restaurant in the strange, black cube-shaped hotel just off the motorway by the Forth Road Bridge is a surprisingly hip, New York style grill. The walls are bare brick, wooden slat details create separate areas, the lighting is kept low, and the menu specialises in succulent steaks and seafood. The speciality cocktail, an aviator, gives a pre or post dinner kick.

TOP NOSH: MICHELIN STAR RESTAURANTS

Edinburgh has five prestigious Michelin starred restaurants, with a cluster found down in Leith. Here are the top restaurants in the city for connoisseurs of fine dining and for those who want to splurge.

The Kitchin
78 Commercial Quay, 0131 555 1755, info@thekitchen.com
www.thekitchin.com
Tuesday to Saturday 12.15pm to 2.15pm and 6.30pm to 10.30pm, closed Sunday and Monday
Tom Kitchin's Leith restaurant fuses rustic seasonal Scottish ingredients with French cooking techniques. A set lunch for around £26 makes it an afford-able place to try award-winning food. Tasting menus allow guests to experi-ence a range of flavours and textures in the sophisticated dishes. Tom Kitchin also owns Castle Terrace Restaurant on Castle Terrace, and Gastro- pub The Scran and Scallie in Stockbridge.

Plumed Horse
50 – 54 Henderson Street, 0131 554 5556, contact@plumedhorse.co.uk
www.plumedhorse.co.uk

Tuesday to Saturday 12.30 to 1.30pm, Tuesday to Thursday 7pm to 9pm, and Friday and Saturday 6.30pm to 9pm

Chef Tony Borthwick has been awarded a Michelin star and two AA rosettes for Plumed Horse, and with a menu of rich meats and desserts it's a satisfying feast for the senses. There's a £69 tasting menu and £55 three-course dinner, but with 40 seats and limited opening times it should be booked in advance.

Restaurant Martin Wishart
54 The Shore, 0131 553 3557, info@marti-wishart.co.uk
www.martin-wishart.co.uk
Tuesday to Friday 12pm to 2pm, 7pm to 10pm, Saturday 12pm to 1.30pm, 7pm to 10pm, closed Sunday and Monday.

It's considered the most prestigious restaurant in Edinburgh, the place you go for that very special occasion, and one that has brought in the Michelin stars and AA rosettes. A six-course set menu for £75 brings to the table such dishes as lobster soufflé, ceviche of halibut with mango and passion fruit, and flammkuchen tart and crispy ox tongue. Wishart also has a cook school in Leith and The Honours restaurant at 58a North Castle Street.

21212
3 Royal Terrace, 0131 523 1030, reservations@21212restaurant.co.uk
www.21212restaurant.co.uk
The numerical name comes from the menu – two choices of starter, main and desert, with one choice of soup and cheese between the courses. The restaurant is set in a grand and opulent Georgian terrace house and chef Paul Kitching creates an appropriately grand menu, which changes every week. It's also the only one of the Michelin restaurants with rooms attached.

Number One
1 Princes Street, 0131 557 6727, numberone@roccofortehotels.com
www.restaurantnumberone.com
6.30pm to 10pm Sunday to Friday, 6pm to 10pm Saturday
The Balmoral Hotel's Michelin restaurant, Number One is styled like a luxurious brasserie in warm tones and with velvet seating. Along with its Michelin star, it's also been named as one of the top ten restaurants in the UK by the Sunday Times. A three-course menu is £68 and there is also a gourmet experience for two, complete with wines and champagne for £250.

Wasabi Disco at Sneaky Pete's, photo Kris Walker

CLUBS

You'll find many of the coolest clubs in Edinburgh located in and around the Cowgate, in the cavernous spaces and chambers under South Bridge, known as the vaults.

Edinburgh residents often lament the loss of several clubs over the past ten years where they could get their fix of techno and drum n bass, which had a large and fairly close-knit following in the city.

A few years ago The Venue, a multi storied home to a number of clubs including Pure, was shut for development in the area. It's now an art space, but if you look closely through the window you can see a sign with graffiti hanging on the wall. It says 'RIP the best', and had been scrawled on the door when it was closed for good.

But there are still plenty of places to go no matter what kind of music you are into. The Bongo Club is the place to go in the city for alternative nights, and then there's the Caves, which is located under the cavernous medieval arches of the Old Town.

The Bongo Club
66 Cowgate, 0131 558 8844
www.thebongoclub.co.uk
The Bongo Club is one of the most versatile of clubs, in a dramatic location under Central Library and with a mix of grime, techno and funk nights. It's casual, relaxed and just a little down and dirty. Because Bongo is run by Out of The Blue, a Leith based creative charity, there are also art events and performances some early evenings.

Some of the nights you should look out for are Big 'n' Bashy, a dub-step, reggae and grime night on the last Saturday of every month, Champion

Sound, a dubstep and drum n base night every Wednesday, the burlesque and glam techno Confusion is Sex on a Friday at the beginning of the month, techno night Substance once every two months and Club Four Corners, one of the busiest nights on a Friday at the end of the month, with reggae, deep-funk, and soul jazz.

The Cabaret Voltaire,
36 - 38 Blair Street, 0131 247 4704
Thecabaretvoltaire.com
Known as Cab Vol or The Cab, it's a typical Edinburgh club space with small, interconnected rooms down steps into a basement, with a more dressed up, ritzier club than the Bongo, but still with some underground dance music nights, and gigs usually from 7pm to 10pm. DM Lovers is on the first Sunday of every month, and pays tribute to Doc Marten boots, with the club dressed up as a house party and punk, reggae, hip hop and pop on the stereo, while Fly, every Friday night, has the best local DJs playing house, bass and garage. You can also hire a booth for pizza and cocktails.

Sneaky Pete's
73 Cowgate, 0131 225 1757
Sneakypetes.co.uk
Hot, sweaty and a bit crazy, Sneaky Pete's has come into its own with some of the best club nights in the city. Once a rough, sleazy club going back to the 1990s, it was revived as an underground venue with some of the best nights in the city. There's something on most nights, but highlights include house and punk night Wasabi Disco on the third Saturday of every month, Nu-Fire every Monday, Numbers and Lucky Me specials and Ride's female DJs playing hip hop and dance on the last Saturday of the month.

Studio 24
24 – 26 Calton Road, 0131 558 3758
www.studio24.me
Dark, dingy and hidden by a bridge under Waverley Station, Studio 24, also known as Calton Studios is an underground, independent club which is home to techno, goth and metal nights, and often taken over

with psychedelia. Anything goes with the dress code, but it's casual, dressed down, and a friendly environment, with a main room and some smaller space upstairs. Balkanarama is a Balkan music rave, Studio 24 Goes Metal is on the last Saturday of the month, and The Bunker is a skate night in an indoor park with ping, pong, live music and projectors, every Wednesday.

The Caves
8 – 12 Niddry Street South, 0131 557 8989
www.thecavesedinburgh.com
Dark and cavernous, with its original high vaulted stonework, the Caves is one of Edinburgh's best venues. If those stone walls could talk they would reveal a lot of history in what's been happening in this converted substructure of the 18th century Cowgate Bridge. There are plenty of rooms to get lost in and it's definitely an experience when the place is taken over by one of the regular in-house club nights including Karnival and Departure Lounge.

The Liquid Room
9C Victoria Street, 0131 225 2564
A music venue and club, with a separate, smaller space known as The Annex, has a variety of different nights. The line-up includes well-known bands, indie nights such as Madchester which offer cheap drinks, techno night Jackhammer which often gets big name Detroit DJs, and some more crowd pleasing house and pop night during the week.

Electric Circus
36 Market Street, 0131 226 4224, info@theelectriccircus.biz
www.theelectriccircus.biz/
Designed to be a neon-lit, Clockwork Orange inspired experience, Electric Circus is an eclectic, glamorous club for karaoke fun. There are karaoke booths to hire out, and it's the type of place where you can hear glam-rock, live indie, Scottish electronica and a David Bowie tribute band in their live music room, as well as upbeat club nights.

The Citrus Club

40 – 42 Grindlay Street, 0131 622 7085

www.citrusclub.co.uk

Found in the West End, near Lothian Road, Citrus Club has been going for over 20 years, with a young, student crowd coming for indie and soul, Tease Age every Saturday is for 1990s indie and 60s soul fans, Planet Earth, every Friday, is a retro club night playing the likes of Bowie, The Pixies and Stevie Wonder, and Bandioke on Fridays is for karaoke with a live band.

The Wee Red Bar

Edinburgh College of Art, Lauriston Place, 0131 229 1442

www.weeredbar.co.uk

Part of the Edinburgh College of Art, The Wee Red Bar features intimate performances and gigs, a popular Saturday Indie night called The Egg, and country and alternative folk nights. It's frequented by a cool, alternative crowd, not necessarily students, but with cheap drinks and the feel as if it's just been discovered off the beaten track.

Pivo

2 – 6 Calton Road, 0131 557 2925

www.pivo-edinburgh.co.uk

Behind red shutters and metal door is Pivo, a Czech themed pub which gets packed out on weekend nights, with a friendly crowd crammed into spaces around the bar, and dancing in the backroom where DJs play. There are benches and leather sofas which get snapped up pretty quickly, and it's also popular as a pre-club venue for eastern European beer and vodka. The outside of its building also featured in the opening scenes of Trainspotting (before it was Pivo.)

Espionage

4 India Buildings, 0131 477 7007

Espionage007.co.uk/edinburgh/

Set within the maize like India Buildings, with multi levels that go all way down to the reaches of the Cowgate, Espionage is a little bit cheesy, but is free to get in and an interesting experience as you explore the different floors, from a ground floor nightclub, to a relaxed Kasbah.

KRIS 'WASABI' WALKER, FOUNDER AND DJ FOR WASABI DISCO AT SNEAKY PETE'S

What's the Edinburgh club scene like?

The Edinburgh Scene has suffered recently due to some significant clubs closures however I feel this has helped re-balance the scene and help install a mindset that it's not all about getting the current big name DJs but more about a value for money good night out. We have a bunch of residents who really know there stuff and most genres are catered for from dub to disco and beyond. It's in a real healthy state at the moment

What's your favourite venue in the city?

Sorry but it's Sneaky Pete's. The 5 years Wasabi Disco has run have been an absolute blast with a consistently warm crowd who are totally up for it and staff that are great banter. It's a tiny sweat box that is purely designed for dancing!

Any local DJs that people should look out for?

So many. Not So Silent have been bringing some really good guests lately. Nick and Gareth at Heavy Gossip / Ultragroove, the Juice, the Playdate and Witness boys at Sneaky's, Substance and Jackhammer for the harder stuff, Betamax is great for 80's Synth, New Wave and Post Punk, and Braw Gigs have been bringing Alternative underground and Avant Garde acts for the last few years, if you want something a little different.

Can Edinburgh compete with Glasgow in terms of its club scene?

It's a well-used question. Not really, as it's very different, but what people forget is Glasgow is better than most cities for clubbing. It's better than Manchester, it's better than Liverpool and it's arguably better than London. But Edinburgh is rocking and you'll not struggle to have a great night out. I think Edinburgh trumps Glasgow in terms of Drum n' Bass, Dub-Step and Bass etc. I've had a fair few Glasgow DJ's play at Wasabi and they have all waxed lyrical about it so we are definitely doing something right!

What would your ideal Friday night involve? (favourite bars to go to etc)

I'm an honorary Leither, I love Leith so I'd probably pop in for a bit of banter with Jonny at the Roseleaf, Nobles is good Craic too, and a hop skip and a jump will get me to Elbow, who also do great food! Swing by the City Café, where I've been frequenting since I was an underager. Check to see what's on at The Bongo Club and inevitably, by 3am, Alan the doorman will be scooping me up off the floor in Sneaky Pete's. Textbook.

The Usher Hall

VENUES

The Traverse Theatre

10 Cambridge Street, 0131 228 3223, boxoffice@traverse.co.uk

www.traverse.co.uk

Founded in 1963, The Traverse Theatre has helped launch the career of many of Scotland's great writers and in the 1970s was a stomping ground for up and coming actors including Billy Connolly, Robbie Coltrane, Simon Callow and Timothy Dalton. Playwright John Byrne and actress Tilda Swinton were heavily involved in the theatre in the 1980s. You can see some of this history with personalised plaques on the wall by Robbie Coltrane and Tom Conti. As well as a strong programme of productions, including plays that deal with Scottish issues, they open the doors with workshops and events. The Traverse bar and café is also a popular place for theatre impresarios, writers and fans.

The Usher Hall

Lothian Road, 0131 228 1155

The Usher Hall has a wide-ranging programme featuring the Royal Scottish National Orchestra, pop and jazz, and comedians including Billy Connelly and Michael McIntyre. They also organise special events such as a Halloween screening of 1920s silent horror movies accompanied by a live organist on their historic 1913 organ.

The Usher Hall was opened in 1914 after Andrew Usher donated money specifically for the city to build a concert hall. The Beaux Arts concert hall has been perfectly preserved, with its ornate dome roof, curved walls and sculpture. The glass extension was built very recently, creating a larger space for the box office, a bar, a café and an event space.

The ghost of the Usher Hall has been sighted by some terrified staff members, and he is said to live down in the air-raid shelter built underneath during the war.

The Royal Lyceum Theatre
30b Grindlay Street, 0131 248 4848
www.lyceum.org.uk
A stunningly beautiful Victorian auditorium with three gilded tiers, red velvet and a large chandelier, the Lyceum is Edinburgh's main repertory theatre, and one of the main venues for the festival.

The Lyceum stages eight plays each year, many by classic writers such as Chekhov, Shakespeare and Arthur Miller over their season which runs from September to May.

The King's Theatre
2 Leven Street, 0131 529 6000
www.edtheatres.com
Most people who had their childhood in Edinburgh will have a memory of going to see the pantomime at the King's Theatre; they stage one every year over the festive season. The King's is a bit more showbizzy than the other theatres, and featuring the big London West End shows as they tour the country.

The King's building is also a fascinating piece of history. It was built in 1905, and Andrew Carnegie even laid the foundation stone. You can still the original Art Nouveau lobby and the Viennese baroque auditorium.

The Picturehouse
31 Lothian Road, 0131 221 2280
http://mamacolive.com/thepicturehouse/
The Picturehouse is the place to go for big-name and up-and-coming live gigs and they also host club nights, including Propaganda, the UK's biggest indie night. The building itself has gone through several incarnations, as a music venue that saw Queen, AC/DC, The Smiths and Pink Floyd take to the stage, and then as a meat-market nightclub under several different guises.

The Festival Theatre

13-29 Nicolson Street, 0131 529 6000

www.edtheatres.com

The Festival Theatre, with its shiny glass façade, is Edinburgh's main venue for opera, ballet and musicals. There's been a theatre in this spot since 1830, first as Dunedin Hall and then the Empire Palace Theatre. In 1911 the building was gutted by a ferocious fire in which eleven people backstage were killed. The ghostly apparition of one victim, illusionist The Great Lafayette, is believed to haunt the theatre.

The Assembly Rooms

54 George Street, 0131 220 4348, enquiries@assemblyroomsedinburgh.co.uk

www.assemblyroomsedinburgh.co.uk

The Assembly Rooms dates back to 1787 when it was used for social gatherings such as the Caledonian Hunt Ball and there are four beautifully preserved rooms, including a ballroom and music hall. At Hogmanay they host a ceilidh, over the festival it's a venue for comedy, music and performance, it can be hired throughout the year for private events and it also houses Jamie's Italian restaurant and Salt N Sauce productions.

Summerhall

Summerhall Place, 0845 874 3000, info@summerhall.co.uk

www.summerhall.co.uk

Summerhall is a creative arts hub with workshops and studios, a venue for exhibitions and performance, and also a place to come for a drink or bite to eat. It was formerly The Royal School of Veterinary Studies, or the Dick Vet, and you can still see the jars of pickled specimens still on display. They host interactive art exhibitions, short film screenings and events including life drawing classes, a drink n draw evening, a ceilidh (traditional Scottish dancing) every Tuesday evening, and regular music and comedy.

The Queen's Hall

85 – 89 Clerk Street, 0131 668 2019

www.thequeenshall.net

A music venue in a converted 19th century chapel, the Queen's Hall hosts classical, jazz, blues, folk and rock concerts, and is a venue for the international festival as well as the Jazz and Blues festival. The Scottish National Jazz Orchestra and Scottish Chamber Orchestra are regular performers, and you can also check out old favourites like Billy Bragg, or up-and-coming names like Stanley Odd.

The Playhouse
18 – 22 Greenside Lane, 0131 524 3333
www.atgtickets.com
The Playhouse is the place to catch popular musicals when they come to Edinburgh. It has the largest audience capacity of a theatre in the UK, although it began life as a cinema from 1929 until 1973. From there it has seen Tina Turner, U2, Girls Aloud (who have a backstage mop named after each of the members), and productions of Les Miserables, Mamma Mia and other big theatre productions. But they don't have metal gigs – apparently resident ghost Albert, who has a bar in the theatre named after him, can't stand it. You can do backstage tours on some Saturday mornings to find out more about the backstage goings on and history of the Playhouse.

The Pleasance
60 Pleasance, 0131 650 4673
Actually an Edinburgh University building, which serves as a student union, but during August, it becomes one of the most bustling of festival venues. The courtyard and beer garden is a place where people gather to meet between shows, catch up with friends and grapple to get a seat while doing some celebrity spotting.
www.eusa.ed.ac.uk

Photo courtesy David McLachlan

David McLachlan, lead singer of Edinburgh band Delta Mainline

What makes Edinburgh such a special city?

Edinburgh is such a special and unique place. In the city you are surrounded by amazing architecture and natural beauty. The history is rich, dark and fascinating. As you walk through the old town it's staggering to think you're following in the footsteps of people like Robert Louis Stevenson and Arthur Conan Doyle. The arts and culture are very prominent throughout the year in the city which means you'll always find something entertaining. As a musician Edinburgh is really inspiring - there is a presence that resonates with the creative community which leads to great art, film, literature and music.

What are the best venues for performing and watching gigs?

I really like The Royal Oak and Sandy Bells for traditional Scottish folk music. The Voodoo Rooms has a lovely space to play in. The Queens Hall is also great and has amazing bands and musicians regularly.

How do you find the music scene in Edinburgh?

The music scene in Edinburgh is really vibrant. There are some amazing bands and songwriters. There are a few bands working on really exciting material that should see Edinburgh's music scene receive more recognition.

What would your ideal Friday night in the city involve?

Edinburgh and Leith have some of the best pubs in the world. We are spoilt for choice. I would take a walk through Holyrood Park and head to Holyrood 9A for a few beers with friends. From there, I would head up the pleasance to The Brass Monkey. The night would finish listening to good music at The Royal Oak.

Where would you go to get some fresh air?

Portobello Beach is the perfect place to get some sea air and relax. The Dalriada and The Espy on the promenade are well worth checking out.

The Cameo cinema, photo C Young

CINEMAS

Cineworld

Fountain Park, 130-133 Dundee Street

www.cineworld.co.uk/cinemas/21

Cineworld at Fountainbridge, west of the city centre, is the biggest cinema in Edinburgh, and with the only Imax screen in the city. As well as showing the big blockbusters, they screen independent films and Bollywood extravaganzas. It's also one of the hosts of the Edinburgh Film Festival in June, showing a wide range of independent films.

Vue Cinemas

Vue Edinburgh Omni Centre, Greenside Place

Vue Edinburgh Ocean Terminal, Ocean Drive, Victoria Dock.

www.myvue.com
There are two Vue cinemas in Edinburgh, one in Ocean Terminal and one at Omni Centre, at the top of Leith Walk. They show all the big blockbusters and current releases.

Dominion Cinema
18 Newbattle Terrace, 0131 447 4771
www.dominioncinemas.net
If you like your cinema with history, then the Dominion, and its listed Art Moderne building, is the place to come. The family run cinema was opened in 1938 and it still has the original foyer and kiosks. You can enjoy maximum comfort with leather sofas to sink into and the option to take a glass of wine or beer into the film. It has four screens, including one very tiny one, which must seat only 20 people. Tickets sell out quickly so it's a good idea to book in advance rather than just turning up.

The Filmhouse
88 Lothian Road, 0131 228 2688
www.filmhousecinema.com
The Filmhouse is a favourite for Edinburgh movie lovers, showing selected new releases, world cinema and old films too. They do themed seasons, such as David Lynch and Woody Allen retrospectives, Italian neo-classicism, or a tribute to Stan Winston, so it's worth checking out their website and downloading the brochure to see what's coming up. It's also the main venue for the Edinburgh Film Festival in June, and there is a popular café and bar, so you can grab a bite to eat before or after, or take a drink into the cinema with you. Oh, and they don't do popcorn.

Odeon Cinema
118 Lothian Road, 0871 224 4007
www.odeon.co.uk
The category B listed Odeon building on Lothian Road was opened in 1938 as the Regal Cinema, which then became the ABC, hosting some of the biggest acts during the 1960s. Beatlemania came to Edinburgh in October 1964 when the Fab Four played at the ABC and fans camped outside. The

Rolling Stones, Freddie and the Dreamers and Roy Orbison also performed at one time. Unfortunately Odeon completely demolished the interior, despite keeping the façade, and built brand news screens.

Cameo Cinema

38 Home Street, 0871 902 5723

www.picturehouses.co.uk/cinema/Cameo_Picturehouse/

Just up the road from the Filmhouse, the Cameo is the oldest cinema in Scotland, first opening in 1914 as the King's Cinema. They still have some of the original features such as the terrazzo floor and one of the box-office kiosks.

The Cameo shows a great selection of the latest releases of international films, arthouse and cult classics. They sometimes do matinee doubles or late night screenings of horror films back to back, for example all five Alien films in a row. The bar has a great vibe, and you can also take your drink into the cinema. Screen One is the biggest and has all the original features and ornate details. There are two other small and intimate screens, with an old-fashioned feel to them.

The Scotsman

Balerno Village Green

The Ogston Hall, between Deanpark Brae and Main Street, Balerno

This free cinema is run by Balerno Parish Church and funded through donations, with staff who volunteer their time to help run it. It was set up as a monthly entertainment for locals, but you can reserve a ticket online or pick them up from Balerno post office or the Mill café in Balerno. You can find out what's on via their website.

http://balernovillagescreen.com/about-2/

The Banshee Labyrnth

29-35 Niddry Street, 0131 558 8209

www.thebansheelabyrinth.com

This pub and club in the Old Town vaults also has a cinema where you can ask them to play one of their extensive list of films, with a selection of 80s classics, some horror and newer films.

Graffiti in a warehouse in Leith

GET YOUR ART ON

Scottish National Gallery
The Mound, 0131 624 6200 nginfo@nationalgalleries.org
www.nationalgalleries.org
Everyday 10am to 5pm (Thursdays until 7pm and during August everyday open until 6pm)
Free entry
Based at the foot of the mound, there are two buildings as part of the complex, both neo-classical buildings. The Royal Scottish Academy, closest to Princes Street, is an independent organisation run by Scottish artists and architects, while the National Gallery is the building furthest back from Princes Street.

The National Gallery houses one of the best collections of art in the world, not only the important Scottish artists including Raeburn, Ramsay and Wilkie, but an extensive collection of early Renaissance and works by Monet, Cezanne, Degas and Gaugan. They also hold blockbuster exhibitions. Newly built underneath the gallery is a restaurant, café and shop which can be accessed via Princes Street Gardens. You can enjoy a drink on the seating on the terrace overlooking the gardens, and the restaurant also has its own little herb garden outside.

There is a free bus that runs between the Scottish National Gallery at the Mound, and the Scottish National Gallery of Modern Art, near Dean Village.
From the National Gallery the bus leaves at 11am, 12pm, 2pm, 3pm, 4pm
From the Gallery of Modern Art, the bus leaves at 11.30am, 12.30am, 2.30am, 3.30am, 5pm

Scottish Gallery of Modern Art
75 Belford Road, 0131 624 6200, gmainfo@nationalgalleries.org
Everyday 10am to 5pm (Thursdays until 7pm and during August everyday open until 6pm)
Free entry
Near Dean Village and about 15 minutes walk from the city centre, the modern art gallery is set in large gardens featuring sculptures by artists including Ian Hamilton Finlay, Henry Moore and Nathan Coley, and a landscaped lawn with water features as designed by Charles Jencks.

The gallery has two buildings – Modern One and Modern Two.

One has early 20th century modernist works including Picasso and Matisse, and a post-war collection featuring David Hockney, Andy Warhol, Lucian Freud, Damian Hurst and Tracey Emin.

Two has changing exhibitions, a recreation of Eduard Paolozzi's studio and his sculpture Vulcan in the café. There is also a library and archives which can be visited by appointment. On permanent display is The Stairwell Project by Turner Prize winner Richard Wright.

Scottish National Portrait Gallery
1 Queen Street, 0131 624 6200 pginfo@nationalgalleries.org
Everyday 10am to 5pm (Thursdays until 7pm and during August everyday open until 6pm)
Free entry
Housed in an 1889 neo-gothic red sandstone palace in the New Town, with an Arts and Crafts interior, the portrait gallery has the paintings and photographs of Scotland's most prominent figures. There are paintings of Mary, Queen of Scots, Bonny Prince Charlie and Robert Burns, and more recent icons including Sean Connery and Garbage singer Shirley Manson.

The City Art Centre
2 Market Street, 0131 529 3993
www.edinburghmuseums.org.uk/venues/city-art-centre
Monday to Saturday 10am to 5pm, Sunday 12pm to 5pm
Prices vary, depending on exhibition

The City Art Centre is a nine story art gallery in a former warehouse which holds special exhibitions, events and a collection of Scottish art which is regularly displayed on rotation. In the 1980s it made its name holding several famous blockbusters including Thunderbirds are Go and Gold of the Pharoes, and more recently their entire space was taken up with the work of Scottish artist David Mach and his exploration of the King James Bible, involving the burning of several match sculptures.

Fruitmarket Gallery

45 Market Street, 0131 225 2383, info@fruitmarket.co.uk

www.fruitmarket.co.uk

Monday to Saturday 11am to 6pm, Sunday 12pm to 5pm

Free entry

The Fruitmarket has a changing display of contemporary art and some innovative exhibitions and interactive works.

One of their commissioned works is displayed as part of The Scotsman Steps across the road. It's an interactive work by Martin Creed, Work No. 1059, where he clad every step in a different coloured marble.

They also have a good bookshop and stylish, minimalist café, worth stopping by for their soup or a cake.

The Talbot Rice Gallery

Old College, University of Edinburgh, South Bridge, 0131 650 2210, info.

talbotrice@ed.ac.uk

http://www.ed.ac.uk/about/museums-galleries/talbot-rice

Tuesday to Saturday 10am to 5pm

The Talbot Rice is part of the University of Edinburgh and their aim is to show thought-provoking exhibitions of Scottish and international works. The Georgian Gallery is an ornate, William Playfair designed neo-classical room of pillars, balconies and a cupula. 17th century Dutch paintings and bronzes are displayed in the upper balcony. The white gallery is a modern space which shows contemporary work.

Sculpture Court, Edinburgh College of Art

74 Laurison Place, 0131 651 5800

www.eca.ac.uk
The Beaux-Arts Sculpture Court in the main Edinburgh College of Art building has displays of antique statues, casts of the Elgin Marbles and works by students.

Dundas Street art galleries
Dundas Street has a high concentration of independent art galleries all the way down, which you could take your time to explore. Worth a look is the Bourne Fine Art Gallery (6 Dundas Street), The Scottish Gallery (16 Dundas Street) which is owned by a relative of Samuel Peploe and has works by Scottish colourists, and the Open Eye Gallery (34 Abercromby Place.)

Superclub Studios
11a Gayfield Square, info@superclubstudios.com
www.superclubstudios.com
A contemporary artist-run gallery, project space and studio which has a DIY approach. They hold open days, exhibitions by local Scottish artists, screenings and there's a good shop selling art magazines and self-published comics.

Out of the Blue Drill Hall
30 – 36 Dalmeny Street, 0131 555 7101
www.outoftheblue.org.uk
Monday to Saturday 10am to 5pm
A creative hub for different voluntary organisations and over 100 artists working from the studio, Out of the Blue holds regular courses including a very popular aerial acrobatics class, and sessions for dance, drama and art. It also hosts exhibitions showcasing local artists, works with young people on community projects and is a venue throughout the year for festivals.

Space Artworks
410 Morningside Road, 07870 799407
Spaceartworksblog.wordpress. com
Tuesday 11am to 2pm, Wednesday, Friday and Saturday 11am to 5pm, Thursday 11am to 3pm, closed Sunday.

A community spirited art gallery, Space Artworks features works by artist with physical and learning disabilities and crafts by professional makers of wood, glass, paper, textiles and jewellery. There is also a workshop space for small groups to work on art and design projects.

Jupiter Artland

Bonnington House Steadings, Wilkieston, 01506 889 900, enquiries@jupiterartland.org

www.jupiterartland.org

Adult £8.50, children and students £4.50, concession £6

Open roughly May to September, Thursday to Sunday 10am to 5pm

Set on 100 acres around Bonnington House near Edinburgh Airport, Jupiter sculpture gardens showcases the work of contemporary artists within beautiful grounds. You are given a map on arrival to explore all the works of art in the gardens. There are water features, a wooden structure by American artist Sam Durant called Scaffold, an interactive room where you negotiate through wood and stone, and a colourful chrome structure that reflects the surrounding woods. It's a very special place and new works are constantly being developed.

Even though its location is quite a bit out of town, you can get First Bus 27 or X27 from Haymarket, which takes you outside.

Paper and wood designs at Red Door Gallery

CAROLINE YOUNG

Make and Do

Edinburgh Contemporary Crafts
59 Home Street, 07816 640 298, info@edinburghcontemporarycraftwork-shops.co.uk
www.edinburghcontemporarycraftworkshops.co.uk
This independently run craft centre holds workshops in various crafts such as jewellery, dress –making, bookbinding, upholstery, screenprinting and illustration. Nine resident makers who specialise in different crafts offer tuition and the sharing of their skills, and there are also day taster sessions to try a bit of everything. Regular exhibitions showcase contemporary crafts by Scottish artists and founder Louise Smith organises various community events and family craft programmes.

Edinburgh Printmakers Workshop and Gallery
23 Union Street, 0131 557 2479
www.edinburghprintmakers.co.uk
Gallery open Tuesday to Saturday 10am to 6pm
Edinburgh's workshop for all kinds of print artists has been running for over 45 years. With government funding, it provides a large workroom and equipment for lithography, wood-block printing and silk screen printing. You could try an evening class, drop in for one of their open days or view the artwork made on the premises in their exhibition space.

The Edinburgh sculpture Workshop
Hawthornevale, 0131 551 4490, admin@edinburghsculpture.org
www.edinburghsculpture.org
Monday to Saturday 9.30am to 5pm
This sculpture centre in Newhaven is a place that offers the facilities and expert knowledge for sculptures. It's a base for established artists as well as offering many free opportunities for beginners, events, exhibitions and, as an extra, the Modern Edinburgh Film School. It all takes place in a new custom-made building, the Bill Scott Sculpture Centre. Tours of the centre can be arranged by appointment.

Doodles Ceramic workshop

27 – 29 Marchmont Crescent, 0131 229 1399, painting@doodlesscotland.co.uk

www.doodlescotland.co.uk

Monday, Friday and Saturday 10am to 6pm, Tuesday to Thursday 10.30am to 9opm, Sunday 12pm to 6pm.

When you look through the window you will people in great concentration as they paint their own pottery. You can choose a mug, plate, bowl, egg or vase to decorate, with a choice of glazes and a design library to get ideas. You can also organise parties with choice of bringing your own food and drink.

Kiss the Fish studios

9 Dean Park Street, 0131 332 8912, johnston_rhona@hotmail.com

www.kissthefishstudios.com

Monday to Saturday 10am to 5.30pm, Sunday 11am to 4.30pm

A creative studio and gift shop in Stockbridge, Kiss the Fish can organise parties and craft events. They specialise in decopatching – where you choose an object from their large selection, and decorate it any way you want. They also run workshops which could include Day of the Dead mosaics, sewing, jewellery and card making.

Stills Gallery

23 Cockburn Street, 0131 622 6200, info@stills.org

www.stills.org

Everyday 11am to 6pn

Stills Gallery is Scotland's centre for photography, with contemporary exhibitions as well as darkrooms, digital production facilities, open access facilities, video production units and equipment for hire. They also host talks, workshops and training programmes.

Gallery Bead shop

14 Lochrin Place, 0131 229 2209

Monday to Saturday 10.30am to 5.30pm, Sunday 12pm to 4pm

Scotland's largest bead shop with over 3000 types, and all the extras needed to make your own jewellery. They also do workshops and classes.

Photo courtesy Eleni Kalorkoti

Eleni Kalorkoti, illustrator and artist

What makes Edinburgh such a great city?

I grew up in Edinburgh, so I'm probably more blasé about its attractions than it deserves, but I have to say that each year I'm still pretty thrilled by the festival. To feel every nook and cranny of the city getting taken over by theatre, comedy, dance, art in all its form - that's an exciting time.

Were you inspired by the city in your work?

My work is often inspired by thinking about a place or time that I've never experienced, so while I was there I was probably daydreaming about being somewhere else! Ungrateful.

As an artist and having studied at Edinburgh College of Art, how did you find the art scene in Edinburgh?

Edinburgh's a very artsy city, though it has to be said, often in quite a middle-class middle-aged way. There are some great newer studio/galleries though, Superclub and Rhubaba among them. And shops like Analogue Books and The Red Door Gallery are full of prints, zines and books to tempt you, many by local artists.

What would your ideal Friday night in the city involve?

The Stand comedy club often has great people performing and, blissfully, a no-stag-or-hen-nights rule. Or I'd have to try and pick between my two favourite cinemas - The Cameo and the Filmhouse.

What are your favourite places in Edinburgh?

The walk from Stockbridge to The Dean and Modern Galleries through Dean Village is pretty magical, and hopefully you'll find a good exhibition to go to at the end of it.

Are there any other local artists you admire?

Matthew Swan, painter, maker, Superclub co-founder. Always up to something wonderful. Louise Smurthwaite and Rosie Walters are illustrators and printmakers who you might be able to catch working away on their beautiful things at the Edinburgh Printmaker's Workshop.

The Writer's Museum, photo C Young

LITERATURE LANDMARKS

This city of contrasts creates an interesting backdrop for literature that goes from Irvine Welsh's Leith and Muirhouse to Alexander McCall Smith's Scotland Street, Robert Louis Stevenson's gothic horror and Ian Rankin's modern crime. Edinburgh's history of being a leader in the fields of medical science and anatomy also form some interesting history, as well as the Enlightenment movement.

The rich quality and diversity of writers is also why Edinburgh became Unesco's first City of Literature in 2004.

The writers' museum on Lady Stair's Close is the best place to start when it comes to exploring Edinburgh literary history. It celebrates the works of the city's big three – Robert Burns, Sir Walter Scott and Robert Louis

Stevenson. On display are first editions of books, manuscripts, and personal items belonging to the writers, including Stevenson's wardrobe made by the infamous Deacon Brodie, said to be the inspiration for Jekyll and Hyde. The building itself dates from 1622 and was the home of a wealthy Edinburgh family.

Maker's Court, just down from the Writer's Museum, has quotation marks from Scottish writers engraved in the stone all the way down the steps to the Mound. There are quotations from Muriel Spark, John Barbour, and new flagstones are added all the time – Edinburgh's very own Hollywood Walk of Fame.

James Hogg's The Private Memoirs and Confessions of a Justified Sinner is a gothic horror that reflected Scotland's Calvinism and the ideas of predestination. Robert is haunted by the devilish Gil-Martin on locations including Arthur's Seat, the Black Bull tavern in the Grassmarket and Greyfriars Kirk. The High Church mentioned in the novel is St Giles Cathedral on the High Street, and the Tollbooth, which was on the location of where the Heart of Midlothian is now, is also mentioned.

William Smellie created the first Encyclopedia Britannica in 1768 in his shop in Anchor Close. A plaque now marks this spot.

Prestigious Ramsay Gardens is named after poet and bookseller Allan Ramsay (1686-1758). He designed his octagonal house on the steep slopes by the Castle, which was given the nickname goose-pie because of the shape.

Kenneth Grahame, author of The Wind in the Willows, was born at 30 Castle Street in the New Town in1859.

Sir Walter Scott was born in College Wynd, just off the Cowgate, and in later life he lived at 39 Castle Street. The gothic Scott Monument, in East Prince's Street Gardens, was built as a tribute to Scott, and it features 64 statues of his characters.

Arthur Conan Doyle was born at 11 Picardy Place in 1859. Studying medicine at Edinburgh University, he was inspired by his lecturer Dr Joseph Bell to create the character of Sherlock Holmes, a master of logic. There's a permanent exhibition at Surgeon's Hall Museum with letters, notebooks and artwork showing a link between Conan Doyle, Dr Bell and the city itself.

Robert Louis Stevenson, author of Treasure Island, Kidnapped and The Strange Case of Dr Jekyll and Mr Hyde, grew up in the New Town. He died at the age of 44 in Samoa from a brain hemorrhage caused by tuberculosis.

Stevenson was born at 8 Howard Place in Cannonmills, and his family moved to 9 Inverleith Terrace, before moving to 17 Heriot Row, which formed much of his writing as he lay in bed as a sickly child.

"My eyes were turned downward to the broad lamplit streets, and to where the trees of the garden rustled together all night in undecipherabe blackness," he wrote.

The lamps inspired him to write his poem The Lamplighter, while an island in the pond of Queen Street Gardens was said to inspire Treasure Island.

A Kidnapped statue on Corstorphine Road depicts David Balfour and Alan Breck, and designed by Alexander Stoddart showing their final parting at Corstorphine Hill, after a 230 mile journey from the Isle of Mull. Stevenson is believed to have stayed at The Hawes Inn in South Queensferry, and he even featured it in Kidnapped.

Infamous Deacon Brodie was the inspiration behind Dr Jekyll and Mr Hyde, and the pub on the Royal Mile, Deacon Brodie's tavern pays tribute to this duel personality rogue.

The Prime of Miss Jean Brodie writer Muriel Spark was born at 160 Bruntisfield Place in 1918, and the ladies of Morningside were the inspiration of 1930s teacher Jean Brodie, who taught at a school modelled on James Gillespie's School in Lauderdale Street in Marchmont.

JK Rowling wrote the first Harry Potter at 9a Nicolson Street, which is now the restaurant Spoons, but was formerly known as The Nicolson Street café. The Elephant Café on George IV Bridge also lays claim to being the place where she drafted the book, as she did some of the writing there too.

Exclusive Fettes College, the former high school of Tony Blair is also believed to be Rowling's inspiration for Hogwarts, with its gothic spires.

Ian Rankin's Inspector Rebus, from his series of crime novels, is a regular drinker at the Oxford Bar, on Young Street. Rankin pops in for a pint every now and again, and he chose the bar because it's both close to the city centre and off the beaten track, and with a cross-section of society propping up the bar.

The Old Town's Mary King's Close in Mortal Causes and Fleshmarket Close, in the book of the same name, were two locations of grizzly murders. The city morgue in the Cowgate features prominently, and Rebus meets his pathologist friend Dr John Curt at the nearby Bannerman's Pub, on the corner of Niddry Street and the Cowgate. As for Rebus' police station, he is based at St Leonard's Police Station, on St Leonard's Lane, near the Pleasance and under the shadow of Arthur's Seat.

Rankin's The Falls was inspired by tiny coffins found at Arthur's seat at the same time as Burke and Hare were carrying out their murderous crimes. These coffins are now at the National Museum of Scotland.

Ian Rankin is from Fife, but he says Inspector Rebus was born from 19 Arden Street, Marchmont – where the writer once lived and dreamt up the stories for his novels. He imagined Rebus living in a flat right across the road, a quiet residential area where he could stagger home drunk.

Alexander McCall Smith conveys Edinburgh's New Town in his books, some consider to be twee but really capture the characters of Edinburgh's new Town – pushy yoga loving mothers, art gallery owners and a cast of real life characters including Guy Peploe, grandson of Scottish colourist Guy Peploe, and owner of the Scottish Gallery on Dundas Street.

Glass and Thompson, a café on Dundas Street, also features, as does the Cumberland Bar on Cumberland Street. Italian deli Valvona and Crolla on Elm Row is also a favourite of Bertie's mum.

IN THE FOOTSTEPS OF IRVINE WELSH

This Trainspotting tour takes you to the haunts of Renton, Spud and Sickboy, from their homeground of Leith, to Muirhouse and onto the Royal Mile.

Starting at 'The Fit ay the Walk', or the foot of Leith Walk, at the corner of Great Junction Street, is the heart of the novel. It's at the Old Central Station, where the novel gets its name, train spotting in a "barren, desolate hanger", like the wreckage their addiction is doing to their bodies. When the book was written, the formerly grand Caledonian rail station had long been closed and was to be turned into a supermarket and pool, Leith Waterworld, which opened in 1992 but has now closed down.

The old job centre, where they were likely to have signed on, was located in the old station building, but again has been closed for some time.

Sickboy lives in a flat at Cables Wynd House, nicknamed the Banana Flats because of its curved shape. This 1960s block of flats is just off Great Junction Street, towards the Shore.

There's a statue of Queen Victoria, which is referred to as the 'Queen Sticky Vicky,' on the crossroads right at the bottom of the walk.

It's here at the foot of the walk, Sickboy barges in front of the "bomber jackets and shell-suits" to get in a taxi to Tollcross.

Tollcross is where Mother Superior lives, dealing to the housing schemes of Sighthill and Wester Hailes in the south west of the city. They get on the number 10 to go back to Leith.

When Renton arrives back in Edinburgh from London, he walks from Waverley Station, out the entrance on Calton Road, up Leith Street and onto the Walk. He passes the Playhouse as a middle-class crowd pour out onto the streets from watching Carmen, and heading to the restaurants across the road. He passes his old flat in Montgomery Street, and then 'former junk zone' of Albert Street.

"The further ye go doon the walk at this time ay night, the mair likely ye are tae git a burst mooth," he says.

Renton swapped his junkie flat on Montgomery Street, back when it was a less sought after place to live, for a flat near Leith Links, so he can get clean.

Leith Links is a large park to the west of Leith walk. It's here that the Orange rally takes place, and further up Easter Road is the stadium, home to local football team Hibs. Spud drinks at the Percy Pub, which is the Persevere Bar, at 398 Easter Road.

Renton used to play football with Johnny Swan for Portobello's local team Porty Thistle at Meadowbank stadium, just off London Street, which leads from the top of Leith Walk.

Renton gets the number 32 bus to Muirhouse as he goes to see Mikey Forrester for an opium suppository. Forrester lives in one of the five story blocks in Pennywell Court, which have since been demolished to make way for new housing.

He crosses through the Pennywell shopping centre, passing "the steel-shuttered units which have never been let and cross over the car park where cars have never been parked." It's there that he has to make an emergency toilet trip into a betting shop in the shopping centre.

West Granton, an area of social housing that overlooks the Firth of Forth, had three blue gas towers mentioned in the book, with the tale of an aunt arriving in Edinburgh expecting to get a house with a view of the castle. Instead she gets a view of the gasworks. Two of them have been demolished, but one structure has been preserved as an example of Victorian industry.

Back in town, and Renton, Spud and Sickboy are on North Bridge on the first day of the festival, where they agree to meet two Asian girls in the pub Deacon Brodies, on the corner of The Royal Mile and George IV Bridge.

Spud and Renton prepare for Spuds job interview over a milkshake and some speed in an American pub on The Royal Mile, possibly The Filling Station.

It's in a pub on Rose Street where Begbie throws a glass over a balcony. Although it's not clear which pub it is, there are lots of traditional pubs on the street, despite the claim in the book that it's only for "areseholes, wankers and tourists."

On the other side of town, on the southside, Kelly works in the Rutherford lounge and bar, where she gets the 'Mark Hunt' prank call. It was at 3 Drummond Street, which is now the Hispaniola restaurant, but still in a unique building dating from 1834.

Further south is the Minto Hotel, where Sick Boy spends an afternoon 'shagging' two American girls.

After meeting Dianne in a club, Renton goes back to her parent's house in Forrester Park, in west Edinburgh. They get on a train from South Gyle station to Haymarket, and browse in a record shop on Dalry Road.

A LITERATURE AND FILM TOUR
OF THE NEW TOWN

The New Town has provided the backdrop for many Edinburgh set films and novels, including Shallow Grave, The New Town Killers and One Day, where love first blossomed for Dex and Emma. It's also home to the characters of 44 Scotland Street, and locations have featured in films including the Prime of Miss Jean Brodie and Jude, starring Kate Winslet.

Take the tour

Start the tour at the bottom of Dundas Street, the steep street that leads all the way up to George Street and the city centre, and is dotted with art galleries and antique shops.

To the right is Henderson Row, home of boy's school The Edinburgh Academy, which was the 1960s stand in for the Marcia Blane School in the Prime of Miss Jean Brodie, starring Maggie Smith as the idealistic Edinburgh teacher.

Keep on walking up Dundas Street, until you get to the next crossroads.

In the novel One Day, Dex's flat was located at 35 Fettes Row, a property number you won't find as it was a figment of writer David Nicholls' imagination. As Emma and Dex hurried down Dundas Street, they could have turned either left or right onto Fettes Row, but my guess would be that he lived on the east section of the street, the leafier side away from 1960s monstrosity Centrum House.

Head west along Fettes Row, as it makes way to a pedestrianised section with newly built stone buildings, before entering onto the old cobbled streets at the base of Howe Street. St Stephen's Church rises up ahead of you.

The 19th century baroque church was used in the film New Town (2008) and was also glimpsed at the start of Shallow Grave.

Walk up Howe Street, past the cosy St Vincent's Bar, the exterior and interior of which appeared in the film Women Talking Dirty, with James Nesbit and Helena Bonham Carter.

Turning right onto North East Circus Place, the black door at the end of the row, no.6, is the flat in Shallow Grave where Ewan McGregor, Christopher Eccleston and Kerry Fox live.

You can do a loop of the opening credits of the film itself, when to the progressive House sound of Leftfield's Shallow Grave, the camera dizzily speeds up the cobbles of Great King Street, turns left up Howe Street, goes down Gloucester Place, onto north west Circus Place, looks back down onto St Stephens Church, then veers left and stops outside a front door on 6 North East Circus Place.

From North East Circus Place, follow Royal Circus Crescent around the gardens, as featured in New Town Killers.

Turn left onto Circus Gardens, left onto India Street which was also briefly featured in New Town Killers, then turn onto Darnaway Street and you will arrive at Moray Place. It's here, near the junction with Forres Street, where Emma and Dex, in the film version of One Day, shared their first kiss as students in front of some of the most romantic architecture in the city.

Head up Forres Street and turn left on Queen Street. On the corner of Queen Street and Howe Street is the varnished wood exterior of historic Duncanson and Edwards Pawnbrokers (38 Queen Street) as featured in the animated film The Illusionist, where a black taxi pulls up outside.

Head down the hill onto Howe Street, and then turn right onto Heriot Row, one of the city's most famed streets and former home of Robert Louis Stevenson. He lived at No17 from the age of seven. His famous poem Leerie the Lamplighter was inspired by the gas lamps lit each evening, which are still dotted along the street.

Heriot Row was also the home of the murderous banker in New Town Killers, although his address was given as the fictitious New Town Avenue.

Heriot Row looks south onto Queen Street Gardens, which featured in Shallow Grave.

Further down Dundas Street on the left side in Glass and Thompson, a café which is a favourite of Alexander McCall Smith, having featured in several novels as well as being the stand in for Big Lou's Café from 44 Scotland Street. Guy Peplo, grandson of Scottish artist Samuel Peplo owns the next door Scottish Gallery, also featured in 44 Scotland Street.

Cross the road onto Northumberland Street, which was transformed into a 19th Century street for the Kate Winslet film Jude (1996).

Take a short cut past the Star Bar and along the cobbled lane at the back of the Drummond Place tenements and through Dublin Mews, onto Dublin Street.

Dublin Street is the setting for the popular 2012 romantic erotic novel On Dublin Street by Falkirk writer Samantha Young.

The route curves around Drummond Place and you get to Scotland Street, which was used for exterior shots in Shallow Grave (1994). It's also the setting for Alexander McCall Smith's 44 Scotland Street, although the street in actuality only goes up to 43.

Go onto Royal Crescent and continue down the steps into King George V Park. There are a number of disused railway tunnels which have become a hub for graffiti art, some pieces done by renowned local graffiti artist Elph, as part of a youth work project.

That's the tour finished, so come back out the park and head up towards Cumberland Street, where you can grab a pint at the Cumberland Bar. In 44 Scotland Street, Angus the portrait painter is a Cumberland regular, while Cyril the dog has his own beer bowl.

Ann Russell, stylist and Frock Trade fashion blogger

What Scottish designers should people look out for?

Holly Fulton is a huge favourite of mine. When I saw her most recent collection at London Fashion Week it took my breath away. I'd happily wear it all! There's also some exciting up-and-coming designers that have caught my eye recently. I love the elegance of Joanne McGillivray, the quirkiness of Deetz and the innovation of Judy R Clark.

What are your favourite independent boutiques in Edinburgh?

I love ALC and Kakao by K on Thistle Street. ALC has a great variety of jeans and offers a really high standard of service. Most women find it really difficult to get the perfect fit so it's great to have a denim expert to hand. Kakao by K has a lovely selection of luxurious Scandinavian clothing that looks effortlessly stylish on everyone! For a vintage fix I'd recommend Those Were the Days in Stockbridge for an excellent range of quality 1930s to 1980s pieces.

If you had 25 hours in Edinburgh what would you do?

Tourists should visit Edinburgh in August to experience the festival atmosphere and plan a visit to the castle, the National Museum on Chambers Street and climb Arthurs Seat for stunning views of the city. As a local I'd have brunch at The Blue Bear on Brandon Terrace then take a leisurely walk through the Botanic Gardens in the sun. After the walk I'd head up to Thistle Street for some retail therapy then pop along to Patisserie Valerie on Rose Street for a huge slice of cake and a hot chocolate. I'd finish the day with a lovely Italian dinner at Nonnas in Morningside and a film at the Dominion Cinema. In the morning I'd wake up to castle views from the Caledonian Suite at the Waldorf hotel.

Where do you go to escape from it all?

I live in Greenbank, not far from the Hermitage of Braid which has some really lovely forest walks. When you're there it's hard to believe you're in the middle of a city. We also like to have Sunday lunch at The Sheep's Heid in Duddingston. The food is excellent and the village is a peaceful place to stroll around. If I'm in the mood to venture further afield St Andrews is a great place for a day trip.

How would you compare Edinburgh style with Glasgow?

I'm originally from Glasgow but have lived in Edinburgh for several years so I've observed style in both cities. I think Edinburgh is definitely more understated than Glasgow. People in Glasgow make a huge effort to dress up on a Saturday night (dress, heels, fake tan, the works!) whilst style in Edinburgh is more polished and natural. Girls in Glasgow aren't afraid to embrace a trend. Both cities are sophisticated in their own right and I like the simple elegance of Edinburgh paired with elements of Glasgow's trend led style.

Beltane Fire Festival

The Edinburgh Mela

FESTIVALS

Edinburgh knows how to put on a good festival. And while the big music festivals like Rockness and T in the Park take place in other parts of the country, the capital city has all the other types covered - arts, comedy, jazz and blues, film, food, and pagan rituals. So here's a guide to the best of the fests across the city.

April
Edinburgh International Science Festival
Two weeks in April
www.sciencefestival.co.uk
A celebration of the wonders of science and technology, with workshops, talks and activities. Past speakers have included one of the founders of Apple, Steve Wozniak, and activities cover the wonders of the natural world, space environment and cutting edge technology.

Edinburgh International Harp Festival
www.harpfestival.co.uk
One week in April
Going since 1982, the harp festival takes place at Merchiston Castle School, with a programme of workshops, concerts, the history of the harp in ancient Scotland, Gaelic music, ceilidh dancing and late evening music sessions.

Beltane Fire Festival
30 April, Calton Hill
Beltanefiresociety.wordpress.com
Tickets are usually around £7 in advance

Beltane, a pagan celebration on Calton Hill, was inspired by the ancient Gaelic festival Beltane which marked the beginning of summer. The Beltane Fire Society is a voluntary organisation with artists and performers who form a procession up Calton Hill and paint their bodies, wear masks, carry torches, and do ritual dances around the bonfire.

Tradfest

http://www.scottishstorytellingcentre.co.uk/tradfest/tradfest.asp

Ten days in April and May

Formerly known as Ceilidh Culture, Tradfest is organised by the Scottish Storytelling Centre as an event that celebrates Scottish music and song, with folk singers, fiddle music, walks and talks across the city.

June

Edinburgh International Film Festival

www.edfilmfest.org.uk

Two weeks in June

Edinburgh's film festival, once part of the international festival, has become a separate entity in recent years by taking place in June rather than August. Mostly centred around the Filmhouse on Lothian Road and Cineworld in Fountainbridge, there is a programme of arthouse, international and big name films, as well as talks and Q & As with filmmakers.

Leith Festival

www.leithfestival.com

One weekend in June

The good folk of Leith come together for a celebration that involves dance, theatre, and exhibitions. The festival supports local organisations, with contributions from the Citadel Youth Centre, local samba drumming troupe Pulse of the Place, a dance tent for raving, and tea dancing if you want to be more civilised. If you want to experience Leith then it's a great way to see the vibrancy and community spirit of the place.

Edinburgh Festival of Cycling

www.edfoc.org.uk

One week in Mid-June

A programme of cycling related events to encourage more people to take up the two-wheeled, green approach to transport. There are workshops on bike maintenance, strength training, bamboo bike frame building, cycle tours up Arthur's Seat and around the city, unicycle demos and talks from famous cyclists. In fact anything bike related that you could possibly imagine.

Festival of the Erotic Arts
One week in mid-June
www.erotic-arts.co.uk
The UKs only festival to celebrate the erotic, fetishist art forms, with erotic visuals and exhibitions, burlesque performance, punky neo-burlesque, workshops in such skills as whip-cracking and the art of seduction. As a festival that is run by women, it has a feminist slant that promotes equality, making it clear that the festival is not about porn.

The Meadows Festival
www.meadowsfestival.org
First weekend in June
An annual celebration since 1974, the Meadows, a huge grassy area in the south side, is taken over with live music, food, craft and car-boot stalls, a funfair and dance demonstrations. It's quirky, alternative, hippyish and perfect for a sunny day.

The Royal Highland Show
Royalhighlandshow.org
A weekend in June
One of the busiest events in Edinburgh's calendar, taking place at Ingleston, near Edinburgh airport, the Royal Highland Show is a farm and country fair showcasing cattle, sheep (and lots of Highland cow), country clothing, motor shows, falconry demonstrations, horse-riding and all those typical country pursuits.

West Port Book festival
Westportbookfestival.org
Four days at the end of June

The West Port, with its mix of independent bookshops, stripclubs and students, could define Edinburgh's literary history – culture, seediness, refinement all merging together. This book festival was set up to compliment the international book festival as a smaller, more independent version.

July
Edinburgh Jazz and Blues Festival
www.edinburghjazzfestival.com
One week Mid July
Jazz and summertime go together like a G & T or strawberries and cream, and this festival celebrates the soulful, funky sounds of jazz and blues with street music in the Grassmarkets, intimate gigs in Tron Kirk, international jazz musicians from New Orleans or Guinea and a Princes Street Gardens carnival with fashion, dance and music. It's sultry, dreamy and inspiring.

Edinburgh International Fashion Festival
Two weekends in July
Organised by former model Anna Freemantle, this is Scotland's major fashion festival that demonstrates Scottish fashion isn't just about tartan. It celebrates established and upcoming designers with runways, exhibitions and parties.

August
The Edinburgh International Festival
www.eif.co.uk
Three weeks in August
The Edinburgh International Festival is officially a separate event from the Fringe (see below), even though it's often seen as the same. But EIF is more a celebration of the higher arts - theatre, dance, opera, classical music, visual art exhibitions and talks. It was started in 1947 as a marker of the post-war period, and the "flowering of human spirit." Big productions take place in all the major venues of the city. The festival culminates with a huge fireworks show over Edinburgh Castle.

The Edinburgh Festival Fringe
www.edfringe.com

August

What started out in 1947 as an off-shoot of the international festival, as a more affordable option for locals to see performing arts, is now the largest arts festival in the world. It's predominantly known for comedy, with many of the big comedians cutting their teeth in Edinburgh, and with regulars coming back year after year. But there is also dance, theatre, music, puppetry, showing in hundreds of venues across the city, taking over bars and pubs, community centres and churches. There are options for free comedy in venues including Espionage, The Three Sisters and The Voodoo Rooms, some shows are just a couple of quid, and you can get half-price preview tickets in the first few days.

There are also festival hubs with beer gardens and beer tents that become a fun, lively base to take in the festival. Spiegeltent in George Square, Udderbelly in Bristo Square and the Pleasance Courtyard just off the Pleasance are three of the most popular, and also offer a great chance to do some celebrity spotting. So download the brochure and plan out your trip!

The Royal Edinburgh Military Tattoo
www.edintattoo.co.uk
Three weeks in August
Every evening for its three week run the castle esplanade is taken over with military parades, pipes and drums representing countries from around the world as well as Scottish regiments. It's been going since 1950 and around 215,000 people see it every year.

Edinburgh Book Festival
www.edbookfest.co.uk
Last three weeks in August
Normally a private garden, leafy Charlotte Square is opened up during August for the book festival, with tents, cafes and a boardwalk all set up within the grounds. The packed three week programme features talks by some big-name writers, which in the past have included Sebastian Faulks, the Wire's David Simon, Salman Rushdie and JK Rowling, introductions to new books, writing workshops by successful authors, and lots of children's events.

The Burry Man
www.ferryfair.co.uk
Second Friday in August
A pagan ritual that has been going every year since at least 1687, the Burry Man parade coincides with South Queensferry's annual Ferry Fair. A man, dressed in a flannel suit entirely covered from head to toe in the burrs of gorse bush, is led through town in a procession where he must have a drink in every pub along the street. It's a bizarre sight, and the burry man gets drunker as the day progresses, supported on either side by two helpers, as he can hardly move or see out of his shrub encrusted suit.

The Mela
www.edinburgh-mela.co.uk
One weekend at the end of August/beginning September
The Edinburgh Mela is a weekend of world music, dance, fashion and food, particularly embracing Asian cultures. Held at Leith Links, it's a riot of activity, with Scotland meets Bollywood dancing, bellydancing, African story-telling, Nepalese masks, and stalls selling ethnic foods, clothing and accessories.

September
Art in the Park
www.colintonvillage.com
A Sunday in September, Spylaw Park, Colinton
A voluntary festival in the village of Colinton, in the outskirts of Edinburgh, which features arts and craft stalls, music and dance performances, food, drink and the general atmosphere of a fun village fair.

Hogmanay
31 December
One of the biggest street parties in the world, Hogmanay involves live music in Princes Street Garden, a large area of the city centre being closed off for a gathering en-masse for wrist band holders, and fireworks over the castle, showing that no one celebrates New Year better than the Scots.

One Spa, photo courtesy The Sheraton

WELLBEING

Union Yoga
25 Rodney Street, 0131 558 3334
www.unionyoga.co.uk
Check their website for class times
Union Yoga offers drop-in yoga sessions – great if you need a session to loosen the joints. There are lunch time drop-in classes for Ashtanga yoga, Zumba, core strength, Tai Chi and restorative yoga. There's even coconut water for sale behind the counter. Good value weekend day passes are £10.

The Yoga Room
5a Forth Street, 07949 266 582, row_warren@hotmail.com
www.ro-yoga.com
With a maximum capacity of 14, The Yoga Room offers a more intimate setting to practice yoga. Founder Rowena Warren was the first Ashtanga yoga teacher in Scotland and she even has a testimonial from Russell Brand on her site. It's an intimate setting, and with its traditional mantel piece, a bit like doing yoga in a beautiful living room.

Glenogle Swim Centre

Glenogle Road, 0131 343 6376 info.gsc@edinburghleisure.co.uk

www.edinburghleisure.co.uk/venues/glenogle-swim-centre

Monday to Friday 7am to 10pm, Saturday 8am to 4pm, Sunday 8am to 4pm

Glenogle Swim Centre, located near the historic Stock Bridge colonies, is an atmospheric Victorian Swimming baths which has recently under gone a refurb. Named by the Independent as one of the 50 best pools, it has kept the unique Victorian features of its balcony and changing rooms by the side of the pool. There's also a gym with new facilities, a sauna and steamroom.

The Commonwealth Pool

Dalkeith Road, 0131 667 7211, info.rcp@edinburghleisure.co.uk

www.edinburghleisure.co.uk

Monday to Friday 5.30am to 10pm, Saturday 5.30am to 8pm, Sunday 7.30am to 10pm

The Commonwealth Pool, known as the Commie, is the biggest pool in Edinburgh, and was constructed in 1986 for the Edinburgh Commonwealth Games. The main pool is 50m in length, there's a 25m diving pool, a gym and fitness classes, and it costs £6.90 to use the gym and pool.

Dance Base

14 – 16 Grassmarket, 0131 225 5525, dance@dancebase.co.uk

www.dancebase.co.uk

Dance Base in the Grassmarket holds drop-in classes in a modern, specially built space, and covering all types of dance – belly dancing, ballet, hip-hop, contemporary, Latin – and all throughout the day. Check their website or pick up a brochure to see what appeals.

Beauty

Charlie Miller

www.charliemiller.co.uk

There are five branches of Charlie Miller, an award-winning Edinburgh hair salon started in 1965 by Charlie Miller OBE, and they guarantee a good hairstyle and specialist colouring in busy but relaxing surroundings. Charlie Millar is also heavily supportive of the charity that creates wigs for teenage cancer patients, the Hair 4 U project.

Cheynes
www.cheyneshairdressing.com
Cheynes is another well-known Edinburgh hairdressing chain and there are seven branches dotted across Edinburgh. The George Street branch has a beauty salon and they do Fizzy Fridays, where you can have some bucks fizz in the process.

The Edinburgh Beauty Quarter
32 Lauriston Place, 0131 221 1770, enquiries@edinburghbeautyquarter. co.uk
Old Hollywood is celebrated in style in this beauty salon near the Edinburgh College of Art. The walls are adorned with black and white photos of Rita Hayworth, Marilyn Monroe, they screen old movies in the beauty rooms and the service is efficient and good value.

Hothead
17 West Nicolson Street, 0131 662 1009
www.hotheadhair.co.uk
Monday, Wednesday and Friday 10am to 6pm, Tuesday and Thursday 10am to 6pm, Saturday 10am to 4pm
This isn't just a normal hair salon, Hothead is on the funky end of the scale, in a room with quirky mis-matched furnishings, exposed brickwalls and Tunnocks wafers and drinks on offer as they cut or colour tour hair.

The Scotsman Spa
1 Market Street, 0131 622 3800
Scotsmanspa.com
Monday to Friday 9am to 8pm, Saturday and Sunday 9.15am to 6.45pm
A futuristic looking pool that is kept at an optimum 30 degrees, arctic and tropical showers, a humid tropicarium, a sauna and steamroom, and a package of spa treatments.

One Spa Edinburgh
8 Conference Square, 0131 221 7777, info@onespa.com
www.onespa.com
Monday to Friday 6.30am to 10pm, Saturday and Sunday 7am to 9pm
Consistently named one of the best spas in the UK by Conde Nast Traveller
amongst others, One Spa at the Sheraton Hotel is – in a word - bliss. It's the best
place in Edinburgh to come for a completely chilled spa session. There's a rooftop
outdoor hydropool, an infinity edge swimming pool with views of the castle, and
a gym but the highlight is their thermal suit. You follow their route through
different heated treatments. involves rock and bio saunas, a laconium and tepidarium and rainforest showers, and an extensive list of beauty treatments.

OMH Therapies
35 Thistle Street, 0131 220 1301, info@OMHtherapies.com
www.omhtherapies.com
Monday to Saturday 10am to 6pm (open until 9pm Thursday) closed Sunday
Somewhere incredibly zen, with a blend of east and west philosophies, OMH
specialises in massage, healing and a range of different feel-good therapeu-
tic treatments that some may consider new-agey - traditional Indian head
massage, reflexology, Filipino migraine treatment, Theta healing and EMO
trance. There's also the chance to take a Sunday course in learning reiki.

Old Hollywood theme at Edinburgh Beauty Quarter

Tunnock's tea cakes and caramel wafer

FOOD AND DRINKS

When people think of Scottish food and drinks, the first thing that comes to mind is usually haggis, whisky and a deep-fried Mars Bar.

Scottish cuisine is not known for its health properties – we have a fondness for grease and sugar, but there is also a wealth of fresh seafood, microbreweries and uniquely Scottish produce. Here's a guide to the best of Scottish food and drinks, some more iconic than quality, and some specific to Edinburgh.

Scottish drinks

Irn Bru
This bright orange bubble-gum flavoured fizzy drink is the most popular drink in Scotland, outselling Coca-Cola. It's sworn to be the best hangover cure, maybe the amount of sugar in it acts as a perk-up, and while Barrs keep the recipe top secret, as everyone knows, it's made from 'girders.'

Buckfast
It may be created by the monks of Buckfast Abbey, but its effect on people is most definitely not holy. Buckfast fortified wine, with its cough syrupy consistency, high alcohol and caffeine content, has a reputation for being the drink of choice amongst teenagers and 'neds'.

Tennent's lager
Tennent's lager is Scotland's national beer, sometimes affectionately referred to as a 'pint of piss' or 'cooking lager'. But it's the beer that is in almost every pub and the cheapest on tap, it's light and inoffensive in taste, and Tennent's

also sponsor Scotland's biggest music festival, T in the Park. There was also the chauvinistic period from the 60s through to 1989 with the Lager Lovelies – scantily clad women who appeared on the can.

Edinburgh Gin by Spencerfield Spirit

If you are going to enjoy a gin and tonic in Edinburgh, then search out Spencerfield's Edinburgh gin, distilled in Fife and bottled in the city. It's distilled in a 200 year old copper pot, with botanicals such as juniper, coriander, citrus peel, angelica and orris root. It's worth buying purely for the Art Deco bottle, inspired by 1920s decadence.

Hendrick's is another Scottish gin favourite, always served with tonic and a slice of cucumber instead lime.

Whisky

And of course, there is whisky. If you want to find out more about the amber nectar, then you could visit The Scotch Whisky Experience which takes you on a tour in a whisky barrel, and provides tasting sessions.

You could also arrange a tour of a distillery or visit the Scotch Malt Whisky Society, 28 Queen Street, which has a bar open to non-members.

Scottish food

Haggis

There's a joke about Haggis – that it's a creature in the Highlands with mismatched legs, so that it can run clockwise. In reality, haggis is a savoury pudding, the 'chieftain o' the pudding race', as Burns wrote.

People often feel squeamish about a dish involving the internal organs of a sheep, mashed up with oatmeal and lots of pepper, but just think about the hidden ingredients of sausages and burgers. It's a moreish, creamy, rich tasting dish always served with neeps, tatties and whisky sauce.

Lorne Sausage

Traditional Scottish breakfasts have gone up-market in recent years, but if you find yourself ordering a breakfast in a classic greasy spoon café, then don't be surprised to see a square, flat sausage on your plate or in a roll. It's called a Lorne sausage, and is a particular favourite as a greasy hangover cure or general morning pick-me-up.

Cullen Skink
Cullen Skink, a common menu inclusion in Scottish restaurants, is a creamy soup made from smoked haddock, potato and onions, three staple ingredients of Scottish food.

Tablet
Tablet is the Scottish equivalent of fudge, but an even sweeter version, if that's possible, made from sugar, butter and condensed milk. It has a crumblier, harder texture which then melts in the mouth. For some tablet made in Edinburgh, try the Fudge House of Edinburgh on The Royal Mile, at 197 the Canongate.

Shortbread
Shortbread is not just the classic Scottish biscuit, but perhaps the best of British. It's a crumbly, sweet, buttery biscuit often served with coffee at the end of a meal. Traditionally its only ingredients are butter, sugar and flour, and would be a Christmas treat, packaged in a commemorative tartan tin with a picture of the castle on it, but now you can get a huge variety of artisan types, often with added lavender, orange peel or chocolate. Try one of Edinburgh's markets to sample different makers.

Tunnocks Teacakes
These kitsch foil wrapped domes of gooey mallow, chocolate and biscuit, are a popular sweet treat in Scotland, and they also do chocolate covered caramel wafers. If you find yourself quite taken with Tunnocks, you could buy a tote bag by designer Gillian Kyle, available in various gift shops.

Oatcakes
Crumbly, crunchy, flaky – oatcakes are a particularly Scottish snack, best served with some Scottish cheese and chutney. They are made from oatmeal and water, maybe a touch of oil and flour, and then cooked on a girdle. Oats are traditionally the staple grain which could survive growing in the harsh

Scottish wilds, and could be made on the move, with a bag of oats and a metal plate. Edinburgh brand Nairns make their oatcakes in their factory near Prestonfield in Edinburgh.

Crisps

Scottish people like their bags of crisps (or potato chips if you are Australian or American.) A good Scotttish brand is Mackie's of Scotland – their crisps are rustic, crunchy and tangy.

Stoats Porridge Bars

A great snack on the move, Stoats Porridge Bars are made in Edinburgh and after starting life being sold at food markets, you can now pick them up in many shops and delis. They are packed with oats, honey, sunflower seeds and berries, and are incredibly filling.

Michael Neave, chef and restaurant owner

What makes Edinburgh such a special place?

Well I've grown up in Edinburgh and the atmosphere of the Royal Mile is brilliant. I live in the Royal Mile and worked on the Royal Mile most of my life, so it's special to me.

Where are the best places to source ingredients?

For meat, John Gilmour has farms down in the Borders and fish from the West Coast. It just takes a bit of time to source it and I think you need to source the people right through to the end, the farmers and their farms, the fisheries - it's time consuming but that's what I do and it's worthwhile.

What would your ideal Friday night in Edinburgh be?

I'm in my kitchen with a busy restaurant to be honest.

What other restaurants do you rate in Edinburgh?

Wedgwood for fine dining and Amber restaurant for a quick lunch.

Where do you go to get some fresh air in the city?

Arthur's seat is a two minute walk from the restaurant and you don't feel like you're in the city when your there. It's great for a lunch break.

Edinburgh's craft beer

There's been a huge rise in the numbers of independent breweries across Scotland, but here are the ones from Edinburgh that you should definitely check out.

Barney's Beer
Barney's Beer is created at the original brewery at Summerhall, the Old Dick veterinary medicine school. You can sample it on draught in numerous bars across the city. Beet beer is the colour of beetroot, while Good Ordinary Pale Ale has a toffee-nutty taste.

Knops Beer Company
They say "no beard is required" to enjoy their ales. Meaning, they make it for everyone to enjoy, not just the beer geeks. Their funky labels were inspired by vintage travel posters, and at their brewery on the East Lothian coastline they create such beers as Musselburgh Broke and India Pale Ale.

Innis and Gunn
Established just ten years ago, Innis and Gunn has become one of the most popular of British ales, and it's also the best-selling British beer in Canada and Sweden.

It was originally created to soak whisky barrels to give whisky an ale flavour, but the beer was too good to throw away.

Stewart Brewing Co. Radical Road
Stewart Brewing Co was founded in 2004, but was originally conceived back in the 80s by 16 year old Steve Stewart and his friends, who made their own home brew to get around the drinking laws. Their beers Edinburgh Gold and Hollyrood have won some prestigious awards. Cask ales that pay tribute to Edinburgh include Chilli Reekie, Cauld Reekie, Edinburgh Festival and Forth Mist, and you can find them in numerous bars across the city. You can also book onto a brewery tour and tasting evening.

BrewDog
Ok, so Brew Dog may be manufactured in Aberdeenshire, but the Brew Dog pub in the Cowgate is a real treat for beer lovers. The company are renowned for pushing the boundaries with their stunts, from producing what they claimed was the world's strongest beer to serving freeze beer in stuffed dead animal bodies, and encouraging a fan to have the Brew Dog logo tattooed on his skin. Beers included Trashy Blonde, Punk IPA, 5am Saint and Alice Porter, which is flavoured with vanilla.

Crabbie's alcoholic Ginger beer
Crabbies, originally founded in 1801 in Leith, has had a bit of a resurgence in recent years. Their recipe, with its four top secret ingredients, is incredibly zingy and refreshing and a good alternative to beer or cider.

If you enjoy the drink so much, you could even stay at the old 19th century stone-built factory – Crabbie's Warehouse on Great Junction Street has been refurbished to create flats, some of which are for holiday rent.

Photo courtesy Andrew Barnett

CAROLINE YOUNG

Andrew Barnett, owner of Barney's Beer, based at Summerhall

What do you think makes Edinburgh such a special city?

It's fantastic visually - there are the hills, buildings and the sea. And culturally there is always something happening in music, art, film, entertainment for me and my kids.

What are your favourite pubs in Edinburgh?

The Royal Dick, which is 10 yards from the brewery, the Vintage, The Roseleaf, Joseph Pearce, Victorias, The Pear Tree, The Cambridge and The Espy in Portobello.

What beers should visitors to Edinburgh try?

Barney's of course. It's Edinburgh's only microbrewery for now anyway, but also fairly local are Williams Brothers, Tryst and Inveralmond.

How do you find operating in the old brewery of Summerhall?

It's fantastic - having a place of work which is also a hub for the arts & other small businesses makes work a lot of fun. As well as being social place to work there are all sorts of collaborations or business opportunities. e.g. Science Festival beer, Techcube beer, and I have great story to tell visitors (I have a brewery late last Thursday of each month).

What would your ideal Saturday in Edinburgh involve?

Getting some fresh air with the kids and the dog, either up Arthurs Seat or Portobello Beach, followed by tea or ice cream, depending on the location. Then getting something to eat in one of the many small, independent restaurants and bars, such as The Dogs, Port of Siam and The Roamin' Nose.

'Techno' chippie, Caffe Piccante

THE BEST CHIPPIES IN THE CITY

Salt n Sauce. That's the way they do chips in Edinburgh, and it's seen as a bit unusual from a salt n vinegar point of view, especially in Glasgow. Edinburgh chippy sauce is a brown sauce concoction made traditionally from Gold Star sauce and vinegar.

If this gets you hankering for some battered fish and chunky chips, not wrapped in newspaper anymore, alas, then here are the best fish and chip shops in the city. And while you are at it, why not throw in a deep-fried Mars Bar, one of Scotland's great inventions. How's this for a slice of fried gold?

The Tailend Restaurant and Fish Bar
14 to 15 Albert Place, 0131 555 3577, info@tailendfishbar.co.uk
www.tailendfishbar.co.uk
Every day 12pm to 10pm
Consistently named as Edinburgh's best fish and chip shop, with a connection to Anstruther's famed award-winning chip bar, the Tailend serves up a supper with a bit of sophistication as a take-away or to eat in their restaurant with a bottle of Scottish ale. They have a wide range of fish which can be battered, breaded or grilled in olive oil; as well as scallops or battered Fraserburgh langoustine tails. At £10, the Tailend traditional fish special is not cheap, but it takes a fish supper to the next level.

St Andrews Restaurant
280-284 Portobello High Street, 0131 669 2850
standrewstakeaway.co.uk
Everyday 11.30am to 11pm

For a fish supper at Edinburgh's seaside, feasting on chips while dodging the seagulls, then you should pay a visit to St Andrews chippy in Portobello. As well as haddock, they have all the classic battered Scottish chip shop goods - half chicken, smoked sausage, scampi, haggis and deep-fried pizza and a donner kebab.

Caffe Piccante
19 Broughton Street, 0131 478 7884
www.cafepiccante.com
Monday to Thursday, Sunday 4pm to 3am, Friday and Saturday 4pm to 4am
Fancy some techno with your fish and chips? Caffe Picannte is the coolest chippy in town, serving up classic deep-fried delights, including the deep-fried Mars Bar served with ice-cream, until the early hours. But what makes it a bit different is the DJ spinning tunes on Fridays and Saturdays. They also have an alcohol licence to enjoy a beer with your fish supper.

L'Alba D'oro
7 Henderson Row, 0131 557 2580, info@lalbadoro.com
www.lalbadoro.com
Everyday 5pm to 11pm
With a name that means Dawn of Gold, L'Alba D'Oro is a Scottish- Italian family business that has been serving up fish and chips since 1975, and as well as the take-away they have an attached pizzeria, Anima. With a collection of awards proudly up on the wall, they were also the first take-away to receive a 4 star award from the Scottish Tourist Board. Their fish changes weekly, often including monkfish and sea bass, and they do a special alla Romana, which is fish breaded with sage and onions.

VINTAGE EDINBURGH

If you want to party in Edinburgh like it's the 1920s, then here are a few ideas for some retro things to do, places to dress up or to learn some new skills like burlesque.

Shop

Armstrongs in the Grassmarket is an Edinburgh icon, selling every type of vintage clothing you could dream of. That musty second-hand smell may mean you will have to wash your finds before wearing out!

Those were the days in Stockbridge is a less cluttered way of shopping for vintage. Every glamorous item has been handpicked from around the world, and there are also some classic art deco jewellery, pieces by Chanel and stylish bags.

Lady JoJo's Boutique specialises in dresses from the 50s and 60s. Petticoats, Joan from Mad Men style pencil dresses, retro swimwear.

Look out for Judy's vintage fair when it comes to Edinburgh every now and again. Check out the website to find more details and dates. http://www.judysvintagefair.co.uk/city/edinburgh/

Get the hair and make-up
Miss Dixie Belle brings pin-up style glamour to Bruntsfield, specialising in burlesque undies, retro-style pencil dresses and vintage hair and make-up. So you could get your hair styled into a 40s pompadour and the hot pout of a 1950s pin-up.

Dance

Burlesque lessons at the Voodoo Rooms

The Voodoo Rooms can arrange two hour classes by Charm School to help you discover your inner Gypsy Rose Lee, and learn the art of tease. It's held either in the Speakeasy or the Ballroom, depending on the size of the group. info@thevoodoorooms.com or phone at 0131 556 7060 to discuss a booking Mistress lessons at White Rabbit

Want to learn about how to work your inner dominatrix? Then check out the mistress lessons at White Rabbit on Broughton Street. They also do burlesque and rope bondage classes. Email shop@white-rabbit-edinburgh.com or 0131 557 6819 to find out about booking a class.

Places to go

Laurison Castle
Pay tribute to Downton Abbey at Lauriston Castle, this perfectly preserved Edwardian villa. It was decorated by the last owner, Mr W R Reid between 1902 and 1919 and you can take a tour to get a sense of upstairs/downstairs by visiting the kitchen, modern Edwardian bathroom and living areas with their collection of rugs, tapestries and antique furniture. They also hold various craft events, walks in the garden and other activities so visit their website to find out more.
www.edinburghmuseums.org.uk/venues/Laurison-Castle

Tea party at the Rose Leaf
You can book a Mad Hatters tea party with a difference at this cool little pub down at The Shore. Instead of tea, they can serve up teapots of cocktails, they provide cakes and snacks all served up on chintzy china and you can also borrow a hat from their quirky collection which are usually hanging up on the wall.

They need 48 hours booking in advance, so contact them at info@rose-leaf.co.uk, 0131 476 5268, www.roseleaf.co.uk

Screen your own old movie
You can hire out the private screen at the Dominion Cinema in Morningside, and screen your own old movies in their intimate cinema, with leather sofas and a bar. Prices go from £19 to £35 per head. Call 0131 447 4771 between 3pm and 10pm for more info.

Claire Paterson, owner of Those Were The Days boutique in Stockbridge

What do you like about Edinburgh?

I think Edinburgh is a really beautiful city. I love that you've got so much history and culture, amazing places to visit and fun places to shop and hang out!

What's your fondest childhood memory of Edinburgh?

I have brilliant childhood memories of going to the pantomime every Christmas Eve at the Kings Theatre. Our whole family used to go together and it was such good fun, plus it tired us out so we would go to sleep and allow Santa to visit!

If you had 24 hours in the city what would you do?

I'd start my day off by going for breakfast at Treacle in Broughton Street to set me up for a day of walking about the city. Then I'd spend my day wandering around the New Town and the Old Town and visit some of Edinburgh's amazing independent boutiques.

I'd start with Broughton Street, then I'd work my way along to Thistle Street and then down into Stockbridge and visit all the wee independent gems in St Stephen Street and on the main road through Stockbridge. Then it would be time for a late lunch, so I'd stop off at the Bon Vivant, or Hamiltons in Stockbridge for some grub and a cheeky wee glass of vino.

After lunch I'd wander up through the New Town and take in all the gorgeous architecture, then have a wander around the fab shops in the Grassmarket and Victoria Street and finish off the afternoon with a post shopping cocktail at the bar in the Missoni Hotel.

I'd then go to Divino Enoteca for a glass of fizz, then onto Monteith's on the High Street for an amazing meal, or maybe to the Witchery if I'm feeling like treating myself!

What would your ideal Friday night out involve?

I love spending my Friday nights in Stockbridge. There are some really cool bars there and it's always a really busy and vibey place. My ideal Friday night would start with cocktails at my favourite bar, The Last Word in St Stephen Street. After a few there I'd head to the Antiquary bar for a few and then onto Hector's or Hamilton's for more wine, and probably some food at some point too!

To get some fresh air, where would you go?

I'd go for a wander along Portobello Beach. It's a great place to walk the dog and have a chilled out afternoon.

The Balmoral Hotel clock tower – an integral location for Hallem Foe

FILM LOCATIONS

The 39 Steps, 1935
Hitchcock's classic film featured Waverley Station and a shot of the Forth Rail Bridge, with Robert Donat's famous escape from the train and onto the bridge.

The Battle of the Sexes, 1959
If you want to see how Edinburgh looked in the late 1950s, then The Battle of the Sexes is worth finding, also for a depiction of past attitudes to women in the workplace.

Threatened by a strong woman in their office, New York business men send her "Somewhere really wild, really remote", to Scotland, "a man's world, where the shortest skirts are worn by man."

There are views from the castle esplanade, over Princes Street Gardens, Lady Stair's Close with a view of the Royal Mile, outside the National Gallery on the Mound, and Holyrood Park steps in as a location for the Hebrides as they cross it by jeep.

The Prime of Miss Jean Brodie, 1969
Maggie Smith played idealistic teacher Miss Jean Brodie, who lives in a house on Admiral Terrace.

The Edinburgh Academy, on Hamilton Place near Stockbridge, was the 1960s stand-in for the Marcia Blaine School. The exterior of the private boys' school has not really changed since Maggie Smith taught her crème de la crème.

They visit Greyfriar's Kirkyard, and it's on The Vennel steps in the Grassmarket, with a dramatic view up to Edinburgh rock, where Jean Brodie says 'observe, little girls, the castle!'

Chariots of Fire, 1981
Oscar award-winning Chariots of Fire was based on the life of Eric Liddell, the Edinburgh-born Olympic champion, who has a community centre in Morningside named after him. The famous slow motion run on the beach was at St Andrews, but it was filmed in various places around Edinburgh, including the church at Broughton Place, the Assembly Buildings on the Mound and the George Heriot's rugby grounds at Goldenacre.

Shallow Grave, 1994
Danny Boyle made his mark in this cult film about young professional flat-sharers, a cool New Town flat, a dead body and a suitcase of money. See the New Town walking tour for details of the dizzying route through the New Town in the opening credits.

Trainspotting, 1996
Despite being a tale of Leith junkies, Trainspotting was mostly filmed in Glasgow, except for the opening scene. To the sounds of Iggy Pop's Lust for Life, Renton and Spud are chased by the Police along Princes Street after shoplifting from newsagents John Menzies (no longer there, but was a few doors up from Boots). They are chased down the steps by the Black Bull Tavern and onto Calton Road, past where Bar Pivo now is, just before the bridge, and where Renton is stopped by the car coming down St Ninian's Row, which is actually a dead end.

Jude, 1996
The film adaptation of Thomas Hardy's novel, starring Kate Winslet and Christopher Eccleston was filmed all over Edinburgh. Café Royale, with its traditional features, was a stand for a 19th century pub, there were scenes shot in Greyfriars Graveyard, George Heriot's School and the glasshouse Botanic Gardens and the quadrangle at the Old College of Edinburgh University.

Mary Reilly, 1996
A little seen Julia Roberts film about the housemaid of Dr Jekyll, Mary Reilly was mostly filmed in a studio, but you catch a glimpse of Regent Bridge from Calton Road, and Carrubber's Close, off the Royal Mile.
Women Talking Dirty, 1996

Helena Bonham Carter stars in a film about the complicated love lives of two Edinburgh women, and you can catch a glimpse of the St Vincent Bar in the New Town, a view of The Shore, Castle Wynd Steps, the Mound, and down Niddry Street.

Sixteen Years of Alcohol, 2003
This grim tale of alcohol abuse mournfully shot the National Monument on Calton Hill, while the Potterrow Tunnel featured in a scene heavily inspired by A Clockwork Orange. There's a scene coming out of a pub on the Royal Mile, which has now been refurbished as Whiski Bar.

The Da Vinci Code, 2005
Famously Rosslyn Chapel featured in Pivotal scenes at the end of The Da Vinci Code, as a place that holds the secrets of the Knights Templar.

Festival, 2005
Festival captures the hectic Royal Mile during August and outside the City Chambers, with its street performers, and flyers being shoved into the hands of passersby. The lobby of the Caledonian Hotel features heavily, there's a racy scene in Armstrongs vintage clothes store, drinks at the Antiquary in Stockbridge and at The Pleasance, Daniella Nardini and Chris O'Dowd on Leith Links and a flat on Abercromby Place is the home for a group of Canadian actors.

Hallam Foe, 2007
The Balmoral Hotel is the landmark of Hallam Foe, its bright clock beckoning to him on a rainy North Bridge, and from inside the tower he can spy on a flat in the Old Town, off Cockburn Street. The entrance to this flat is next to Whiplash Trash on Cockburn Street, while the staff entrance to The Balmoral is actually the entrance to the Caledonian Hotel on Rutland Street. He runs from the police up Fleshmarket Close, and down the Scotsman Steps.

New Town Killers, 2008
This fast paced game of cat and mouse takes place all around Edinburgh's city centre and on the housing schemes of Muirhouse. If you know Edinburgh

CAROLINE YOUNG

well, you realise the disjointedness and how it would be impossible to go into the Café Royal and come out in the city centre or in Muirhouse. There's also a chase scene in the Innocent Railway Tunnel, and Dougray Scott's flat is at Herriot Row.

Outcast, 2009
This horror film starring James Nesbitt was filmed at Sighthill, a housing estate in south west Edinburgh, in the empty 1960s tower blocks just before they were demolished to make way for new housing.

The Illusionist, 2010
Beautiful animated film The Illusionist was partly set in Edinburgh, creating a romantic vision of the city from day's gone by. Some of the places depicted included Princes Street and Jenners, The Mound and Edinburgh Castle, George Street, Salisbury Crags of Arthur's Seat, Waverley Station and North Bridge.

The Awakening, 2010
British horror film The Awakening is set in a haunted English boarding school, with Marchmont House in the Scottish Borders standing in for the school, grand, Grecian inspired St Bernard's Crescent in Stockbridge for some city street scenes.

Burke and Hare, 2010
John Landis' comedic telling of the infamous body snatchers was mostly filmed on a soundstage, but there were some location shots in Old Fish Market Close, the University of Edinburgh Anatomy Museum Heriot Place, the cobbled lane with the view of the castle in the background.

One Day, 2011
Romantic One Day was bookmarked by scenes set in Edinburgh. The opening graduation scenes of the 1980s took place in the Old College quadrangle of Edinburgh University. The group walk up North Bridge, along West Bow, the terrace above Victoria Street, and down Warriston Steps and onto Cockburn Street. They kiss on the corner of Forres Street, no. 80 Queen

Street visible in the background. The final scenes are set on the wild slopes of Arthur's Seat, with the views across the city.

The Angels' Share, 2012
Ken Loache's feel-good comedy drama is about a bunch of community service reprobates who plot to steal a bottle of priceless whisky. While it's mostly set in Glasgow but there were a few scenes set in Edinburgh.

There's the view of the Castle as the gang walk along the Princes Street Gardens side of Princes Street to the Caledonian Hotel, where they are taking part in whisky tastings at the Pompadour Rooms.

Cloud Atlas, 2012
The outside of the City Chambers on the Royal Mile was turned into a hotel, St Ninian's Row off Calton Road was transformed into a 1920s street scene, and the mighty Scott's Monument has an important scene, and is also name-checked.

Take a picnic to the Meadows with goodies from Ian Mellis

LAZY SUNDAYS

So you've have a big Saturday night out in Edinburgh, and need some recovery time on a Sunday. Here are some ideas to get the blood circulating once again - maybe a hair of the dog, or for some walking and cycling in the fresh air.

The Turkish baths in Portobello
57 Promenade, Portobello, 0131 669 6888, info.psc@edinburghleisure.co.uk
Open 9.30am to 7pm on Sundays, and for the bargain price of £7, the Turkish baths in Portobello Swim Centre are good for some relaxation. There are three hot rooms of varying temperatures (a tepidarium, calidarium and laconium), a frigidarium for cooling down, a steamroom and a cold plunge pool, all designed to invigorate the body and relax the muscles.

The Stand Comedy Club– Free comedy at lunchtime
5 York Place, 0131 558 7272
www.thestand.co.uk

The Stand Comedy Club does a free Sunday lunchtime improvisation with Stu and Garry, who have been working as a comedy duo for over twenty years. There's no need to book, but a queue starts to form outside before doors open at 12.30pm, ready to order the nachos and burgers before the comedy starts. It's fast-paced, funny and even though it's interactive, they take the piss out of each other rather than the audience.

Stockbridge Market
Every Sunday from 10am to 5pm on the corner of Saunders Street, Stockbridge market is great for buying local artisan products, or sampling the food on offer. There's always the inviting smell of hot meats and curries in the air, and sometimes there is live music.

Walk through Holyrood Park to the Sheep Heid Inn
Take an amble through Holyrood Park to The Sheep's Heid in Duddingston, for their Sunday roast. The pub is the oldest in Edinburgh, and is a cosy, intimate place to unwind. The Sunday roast has platters of roasted meats, Yorkshire puddings, roast potatoes, gravy and then the option of playing board games for afters.

Take an art lesson
Dr Sketchy's Anti-Art School at the Jazz Bar on Chambers Street, is on the second Sunday of the month from 3pm to 6pm, where a burlesque model or a circus performer in fabulous costumes pose for the audience to sketch. It's an idea that was born in New York and happens all over the country.

Take a trip to the Pentlands Hills, and after following one of the walking trips, treat yourself with a pint at the Flotterstone Inn. (see the outdoors section for more details),

Have a picnic to the Meadows.
Stock up on cheese from Ian Mellis, maybe some sausages from Crombie's to barbeque, artisan breads from a local bakery and find a pleasant spot in the Meadows for a Sunday afternoon of relaxation.

Explore the Water of Leith

You could drop in on some sections of the Water of Leith, running from the Pentlands to the Shore, or cover the whole 35km by bike, cycling through the villages of Balerno and Currie in the south west of the city. One of the best sections to join is near the clock at Cannonmills on Brandon Terrace, or going down the steps by Pizza Express in Stockbridge.

Tupiniquim – a gluten-free Brazillian food stall

STREET FOOD

Many of Edinburgh's old blue police boxes, which were set up as community policing outposts, have been converted into cafes and snack stalls. You'll see a number of the maroon boxes across the city, crammed with coffee machines, cups, syrups and beans.

There are also plenty of markets in Edinburgh at the weekends to try some tasty local produce.

Chimney Cake
Middle Meadow Walk, just off Lauriston Place
This Hungarian food stall in the Meadows sells traditional Kurtos Kalacs, or chimney cake, because of their hollow tube like structure, flavoured with cinnamon.

Tupiniquim
The Green Police Box, Middle Meadow Walk
tupiniquimofedinburgh@yahoo.com
A husband and wife team from Sao Paolo deliver gluten-free, healthy Brazillian food to passersby at the Meadows from their colourful converted police box. Crepes are served sweet or savoury, with fruit in caramel, black beans and spiced chicken are some of the hearty fillings, and smoothies are cycle powered from their juice bike and they serve up traditional feijoada on Saturdays.

Elephant Juice food company, George Square
www.elephantjuice.com
Following the street food movement, Elephant Juice trades from an old-fashioned van (Dumbo 1) in George Square, with the promise that "for every

meal you buy, Elephant Juice will feed a hungry person in need." They do healthy porridge for breakfast, soups packed with veg and spices for lunch and hearty casseroles for dinner, so it's ideal for food on the move and with a conscience.

Markets

Edinburgh Farmers Market
Castle Terrace
Every Saturday 9am – 2pm

Edinburgh Market, City Centre
St Mary's Cathedral, Cathedral Lane, beside John Lewis
Saturdays 11am to 5pm

Portobello market
Brighton Park, Portobello
The first Saturday of every month, 9.30am to 1.30pm

Stockbridge Market
Saunders Street
Every Sunday 10am to 5pm

Edinburgh Market, Southside
By the Royal Commonwealth Pool, Dalkeith Road
Sundays 10am to 4pm

ACKNOWLEDGMENTS

Thanks to Andrew Lownie and David Haviland at Thistle Publishing for making this book possible, and to Martina Salvi for her beautiful images.

Thanks also to Tara Nowy, Eleni Kalorkoti, David McLachlan, Michael Neave, Claire Paterson, Kris Walker, Ann Russell and Andrew Barnett for their contribution.

Printed in Great Britain
by Amazon